Everything You Need to Know About Saving For Retirement

BEN CARLSON

CONTENTS

INTRODUCTION: YOU'RE ON YOUR OWN

A staggering 10,000 Baby Boomers are turning 65 years old on a daily basis from now until well into the 2030s. That's nearly four million people reaching retirement age annually in the United States. The vast majority of them are ill-prepared for this next stage of their financial lives. Half of all people aged 55-61 in the United States have less than $21,000 saved for retirement. For Americans in the 50-55 age range, half have less than $11,000 in retirement savings. Half of all families in this country have no retirement nest egg to speak of. One-quarter of senior citizens rely exclusively on Social Security to fund their spending needs in retirement while roughly 50% of seniors get at least half of their retirement income from the program.

Young people aren't doing much better. More than 40% of those in the 18-29 age bracket have nothing saved for retirement. And those in the 25-44 age bracket have seen their wealth decline as a group anywhere from 25% to 50% when compared to people in the same age range in 1989. In 1990, people under the age of 40 owned 13% of the U.S. stock market. By 2020, that ownership percentage was down to 4%. Millennials also have lower incomes and net worth, on average, than their parents did at the same age.

The causes for these financial issues could be its own book but here are four reasons there is a retirement crisis looming for a large number of people in the United States:

Problem #1. Retirement is still a relatively new concept.

Just 34% of all males lived past their 65th birthday in the year 1870. And for those who did, the vast majority of them still worked, often in back-breaking jobs. The labor force participation rate was an astonishing 88% for those in the 65 to 75 age group back when

Ulysses S. Grant was president. About half of all people who lived into their 80s still worked because there was no such thing as retirement for most people.

If you were lucky, retirement might have lasted two to three years towards the end of the 19th century. Most people's retirement plan was, well, death. As more people began living well beyond their mid-60s, retirement as a concept was born. If your parents or grandparents lived through World War II, it's likely they were the first ones in your family to think about retirement as we think about it today. The first wave of retirees had a much different financial arrangement than we have today. Many retirees from previous generations could look forward to collecting a pension and having their healthcare costs covered by their employer in retirement. This is not the case anymore.

There is a double-edged sword of the newfound longevity in the human race. On the one hand, advances in healthcare and technology means most people get to enjoy their time on this planet with loved ones far longer than our ancestors. On the other hand, we now have to make our money last much longer than ever before. When Social Security was first introduced in the 1930s, it was meant to last a handful of years for the majority of recipients. The average time spent in retirement from 1960-1990 was roughly 13 years. It's now over 20 years on average, which means for a large percentage of the retired population it's much longer than two decades.

Since the concept of retirement is still relatively new, there are few role models that can prepare you psychologically or financially for this stage in life. Personal finance is one of the most important life skills you can develop yet no one is tasked with teaching you how to do it. Just six states require students to take at least one semester of personal finance courses. They teach other languages in our schools but not the language of money. Most people are flying blind and you only get one shot at the retirement planning process.

Problem #2. You're on your own.

When Congress passed the Revenue of Act of 1978 to lower tax brackets on individuals, no one could have imagined how it would structurally change the way Americans save for retirement. Deep within this two-hundred-plus page document was a short 900-word section which was added with the intent of limiting executive compensation (Spoiler alert: It did not have that effect).

Ted Benna, an insurance consultant at the time, realized this part of the tax code could be used for both employee and employer retirement contributions in a tax-deferred manner. Benna's discovery was initially used by banks as a way to transfer bonuses to employees in a tax-efficient manner but other companies slowly came around to the idea of a tax-deferred workplace retirement option for their employees. Thus, the defined contribution 401(k) retirement plan was born.

It's a stretch to say *everyone* was once covered by a pension plan but the numbers were much higher for previous generations. In the early-1980s roughly 60% of all workers in the United States could bank on receiving a pension. Today, that number is closer to 17% and heading lower. Now the majority of workers rely on a 401(k) or other defined contribution retirement plan that they're forced to manage and fund on their own.

In the early days, roughly 50% of employees were offered access to this type of plan with hopes of reaching a 95% penetration rate. Instead, less than half of all workers are covered by workplace retirement plans today. Just one-third of all U.S. workers are saving in a 401(k) or similar plan.

With fewer pensions and a general lack of personal finance education, you're on your own when it comes to saving and planning out your retirement and not enough people are doing so.

Problem #3. This stuff is simple but not easy.

Golf is simple. All you have to do is line up your stance, bend your knees, take the club back slowly, follow-through and keep your head down while hitting a little white ball. Getting in shape and losing

4

weight is simple. All you have to do is exercise on a regular basis and eat healthy. Building wealth is also simple. Just live below your means, save the difference and invest for the long term.

Many aspects of life can be boiled down to simple principles or steps. So why isn't everyone a scratch golfer walking around with six-pack abs and fabulously wealthy? Because simple is not the same thing as easy. Legendary golfer Bobby Jones once said, "Golf is played mainly on a five-and-a-half-inch course, the space between your ears." Dieting and exercise each require an extraordinary amount of willpower and discipline. And getting your finances in order is more difficult than it seems because money impacts so many different aspects of your life.

Getting ahead in life is never as easy as a list of life hacks or motivational quotes set against a beautiful backdrop on Instagram. Saving for retirement is simple but it's also exceedingly difficult in that delaying gratification is no fun. Former President Dwight Eisenhower once talked about how he would prioritize his presidential duties after getting elected:

> *I have two kinds of problems: the urgent and the important. The urgent are not important, and the important are never urgent.*

Financial problems that are important - retirement planning, saving, budgeting, etc. - are easy to ignore because they don't become urgent until it's too late. Instead, there's a long list of minor items you can check off your list that make you feel like you've accomplished something in the short-run, even if they don't help you to get ahead over the long-run. It's far easier to focus on the short-term and ignore the long term when you don't have an overarching plan in place to guide your actions.

Problem #4. We're all human.

Most people enjoy learning about personal finance about as much as they enjoy getting a colonoscopy. Sure, people care a lot about money, but few people are interested in the actual nuts and bolts of personal finance or financial literacy. People want to learn how to get rich, not how asset allocation or tax-deferred retirement accounts work. People want to make a handful of decisions about their finances and move on with their lives, not pay attention to this stuff on a regular basis. It's perfectly normal if finance doesn't interest you, but that doesn't mean you can ignore this stuff and hope your finances magically improve on their own.

One of the reasons it's so difficult to get your finances in order is your views on money management can be clouded by your circumstances, family history with money, beliefs, culture and personal experiences. It's nearly impossible to be objective about your own deficiencies because we humans are not objective when it comes to things we care deeply about.

A ground-breaking study performed by Albert Hastorf & Hadley Cantril illustrates why this is the case. These researchers studied the reaction of the fans at an Ivy League football game in November 1951 between Princeton and Dartmouth. The rivalry game was the last of the season for both teams so it got testy from the opening kick-off. The refs were busy throwing flags and penalizing both teams all game. Princeton's star player left the game with a broken nose. A Dartmouth player was carted off with a broken leg. Tempers flared on both sides and the coaches and players did a lot of finger-pointing after the game (which Princeton won) to place blame for the chippy play.

One week after the game was played the researchers asked the students in attendance which team was more responsible for the dirty play. Even when the students were given a video of the game to re-watch what actually happened, each of the student sections came away with different conclusions about what transpired. Princeton students determined Dartmouth players were responsible for twice as many infractions as their team while Dartmouth students felt both sides were to blame. Both groups watched exactly the same game but walked away with entirely different conclusions about what transpired. The truth in these matters is almost always a shade of gray but we see the world in black and white.

What does this mean for your retirement savings? **People are not objective when it comes to decisions or events that involve emotions and money is one of the most emotionally sensitive issues on the planet.** Financial market history, statistics, spreadsheets and probabilities can all be helpful when crafting a financial plan but these topics are all pointless if you don't understand yourself and the psychology of behavior and decision making. Inside all of us is a lesser version of ourselves just waiting to screw up our financial decisions. They're called blind spots for a reason -- we can't see them in ourselves.

And there is nothing wrong with emotions. Emotions are what make us human. Financial writer Jason Zweig once wrote, "My own view is that people are neither rational nor irrational. We are human. We don't like to think harder than we need to, and we have unceasing demands on our attention."

That's the rub for most normal people trying to save for retirement. You have other stuff to worry about. You have a job. You have a family. You have a social life. You have shows to binge watch. You have better things to do than spend all of your time and effort trying to figure out your finances.

So I'm going to keep things simple and walk you through the things a normal person needs to understand about saving and investing for retirement. There are three big things you need to get right in order to give yourself a chance at financial independence one day:

1. Save at least 10% of your income (preferably 15%-20%)
2. Make your saving and investing automatic
3. Think and act for the long term

These three things won't make you rich overnight. They are simple, not easy. They require systems, not tactics. And they are boring, not sexy. The hardest part of this equation is it will be very easy to get off-track.

The goal of this book is to help remove some of the stress,

confusion, and anguish involved in the process. This stuff is not always easy but I am going to try to make it as painless as possible so you can make a handful of big decisions, have a better understanding of your options and allow you to move on with your life so you can focus on more important things and let your money do the work for you.

CHAPTER 1.
WHY YOU NEED
TO SAVE

Brothers Dick and Mac McDonald opened up a drive-in restaurant in the 1940s modeled after a hot dog stand they frequented in San Bernardino, CA. By the late-1940s they decided to reorganize the business to take advantage of some lessons learned and the changing dynamics in the country. The McDonald brothers recognized the burgeoning middle class in America following WWII was moving to the suburbs and feeling more rushed than ever because of their commutes and growing families. People wanted their food faster, so the brothers mechanized the food prep process by turning their kitchen into an assembly line and focusing exclusively on burgers, fries and shakes. This was the invention of fast food and a little restaurant you may have heard of called McDonald's.

Ray Kroc was a milkshake machine salesman who saw potential in the business model, eventually maneuvering his way into a job as the restaurant's franchise agent in 1954 to expand their reach. The McDonald brothers were not in the empire building business, but Kroc was, so he eventually bought them out and helped turn McDonald's into one of the most well-known brands on the planet. Many years later, Kroc was asked why he partnered and then bought out the McDonald brothers when he could have simply copied the system they created. Part of it was the fact that it was by far the best operation Kroc had ever seen of the thousands of kitchens he'd frequented over the years as an appliance salesman. But it was also the name itself that mattered. McDonald's sounded right to him while a chain named Kroc's didn't have the same appeal.

The connotations we place on certain words can change how people feel about them just like McDonald's versus Kroc's. The Big Mac rolls off the tongue a little easier than the Big Kroc.

Saving money is like the Kroc's of personal finance because so many experts evoke terms like 'frugality' and 'delayed gratification' when explaining its merits. Frugal is just another word for cheap and no one wants to be labeled a cheapskate. And delaying gratification sounds awful when you can simply take your gratification now. Saving needs to hire a new advertising firm.

Here's how Don Draper might market the idea of saving money: It buys you the most valuable asset in the world - time. **Time is the most valuable resource on the planet and the only asset where there is no inequality.** We all have a finite amount of time in any given day to work with. Saving money can give you more control over how you spend your time in the future. Time to spend doing what you love. Time with your family and friends. Time spent traveling to exciting destinations. Time not spent going to the office anymore.

Saving allows you to do what you want in the future without having to worry as much about the financial aspects of your decisions. Saving more now means replacing less of your current income when you finally become financially independent. A higher savings rate automatically means a lower spending rate. They go hand-in-hand. Saving is your front-row ticket to financial freedom.

Saving not only frees your time in the future but also gives you a buffer in the present. **Saving money provides a margin of safety when life inevitably gets in the way of your best laid plans.** Life is stressful enough on its own but adding financial problems can amplify the rough patches. The last thing you want to worry about when life throws you a curve ball is money. Money issues amplify stressful situations.

The problem is most people don't dig deep enough when figuring out why they should save in the first place. Getting rich sounds like a reasonable answer but living a rich life means different things to different people. A specific number doesn't make you rich. If you're constantly stressed out about money, it doesn't matter how much you have, you aren't rich if money still makes you worry. Spending money may lead to a short-term burst in happiness but the thrill from buying material possessions wears off fairly quickly.

Saving for retirement sounds impossible to some and too far off in the future for others. If you think about your savings in terms of buying units of time or freedom as opposed to units of money, it can help frame the decision into the proper context. Most people want to get rich but we would all be better off trying to not die poor, or better yet, defining what being rich means on your own terms.

Don't worry if you haven't gotten started yet. All it takes is some small wins to get the ball rolling.

CHAPTER 2.
THE POWER OF
SMALL WINS

A lot of advice that comes from personal finance experts is borderline condescending.

Why don't you just spend less than you earn and save the difference?

Why don't you just stop buying lattes from Starbucks every day?

Do you know how much you could save if you just gave up your Netflix subscription?

Just put your money in the stock market and don't touch it. It's simple!

There is a reason most financial advice doesn't work - it makes people feel bad about themselves. All financial advice sounds simple until you actually try it. Your finances can and should be simplified but they are never easy because of the human element. There are so many choices to make that people can become overwhelmed. It's difficult to know where to start, which accounts to open, which investments make sense and what to do with your money when you finally make the decision to save. And for many, simply coming to that decision can be the hardest part of the process.

I'll start saving when I'm ready.

Save money!? In this economy!?

What's the point of saving money when the system is rigged against me?

Have you seen interest rates lately? What's the point?

It's understandable people are often so overwhelmed that they ignore their finances or focus so intently on the minutiae that they never get started in the first place. But just getting started is the key because small wins can help you train your brain to see positive results that can be turned into lasting habits.

When swim coach Bob Bowman began working with legendary

swimmer Michael Phelps to prepare him for the Olympics, they experimented with the idea of starting small to get Phelps in the right mindset. Bowman told author Charles Duhigg, "Eventually we figured out it was best to concentrate on these tiny moments of success and build them into mental triggers. We worked them into a routine. There's a series of things we do before every race that are designed to give Michael a sense of victory."

The idea is giving yourself a sense of victory helps you see progress which in turn sets in motion a compounding of other small wins that eventually turn into a routine that can make you successful and turn into big wins.

The same is true when you're just starting out as a saver. A team of researchers set out to help people save more money using the power of small wins. They discovered consumers were more likely to save when the decision was framed in terms of putting away $5 a day versus $150 a month. These numbers are basically identical but more than four times as many people agreed to save $5 a day than those who promised to put away $150 a month. How you frame these decisions can have just as big of an impact as the numbers used in your planning calculations. This same principle applies to paying off your debts. Once you get the ball rolling these things begin to snowball in your favor.

My first job out of college paid $36,000 a year. After paying for rent, saving up for an engagement ring, paying back student loans and having a car payment for the first time in my life, there wasn't much room leftover in my budget to save for retirement. The small firm I worked for didn't have a 401(k) plan so after a year or so on the job I opened up an IRA to begin my retirement savings journey. Since I couldn't afford much I put just $50 a month into a target date fund at one of the low-cost fund companies. It wasn't much money and it took a very long time to see results. But I took pride in the fact that I even opened up the account and soon it began to grow.

Over time as I made more money I slowly increased the amount saved. Every time I received a raise I would bump up my savings rate to avoid lifestyle creep and help juice my savings. It took many years to get my savings rate where I wanted it to be. Making a higher income over time certainly helped but the best thing I ever did to build good financial habits was just getting started. Those initial small wins set the tone to get where I eventually wanted to be in terms of saving because it helped develop the correct habits.

James Clear shows the power of minor improvements in his book *Atomic Habits*:

> *The difference a tiny improvement can make over time is astounding. Here's how the math works out: if you can get 1 percent better each day for one year, you'll end up thirty-seven times better by the time you're done. Conversely, if you get 1 percent worse each day for one year, you'll decline nearly down to zero. What starts as a small win or a minor setback accumulates into something much more.*

Getting just 1% better a day would make you 37 times better over the course of the year. This is easier said than done but it shows how tiny improvements can have big results over time. No one starts out training for a marathon by running 26.2 miles on day one. The same is true for your savings.

Let's say you start out saving 3% of your income with a goal of steadily increasing that rate in the future. If you go from saving 3% of your income in year one to 4% in the next, that's a 33% increase in your savings rate. Go from 4% to 5% and you've given yourself a 25% annual jump in savings. Getting to 6% from 5% is a 20% jump. The goal when you're just getting started is to see an increase in your savings rate each year that is bigger than the historical return on the stock market (which has averaged 8% to 10% returns over the past 90 years or so) until you reach your steady state savings rate (more on this in Chapter 5).

It's also important to start building good habits when you're young to lessen the sting of saving more when you're older. Psychologists have determined losses sting twice as bad as gains feel good. If you wait to start saving when you're older it will feel like lost income if those savings habits haven't been developed yet. Therefore, saving money will make you feel twice as bad later in life because it will feel like you're giving yourself a reduction in income.

Early on in your financial lifecycle, the vast majority of your gains will come not from your investing prowess but from your savings rate.

The next chapter will show you why.

CHAPTER 3.
WHEN SHOULD YOU
START SAVING?

As Warren Buffett was closing in on his 60th birthday in 1990, his net worth was close to $4 billion according to the Forbes 400 list. Thirty years later as Buffett hit age 90 in 2020, his net worth skyrocketed to more than $70 billion (and that's after he gave away tens of billions to charity). That means nearly 95% of Buffett's net worth was created after his 60th birthday.

I'll come back to this after we go through a simple example.

Most retirement calculators offer you fairly simple inputs. You enter in the amount you currently have saved, your future saving projections and a return assumption. Then the calculator spits out a future value based on those assumed inputs.

This isn't a perfect way to determine exactly how much money you will have saved up by retirement because life doesn't work in a straight line. Retirement calculators are clean while the real world is messy. Retirement planning is more about accuracy (in the ballpark) than precision (on the bulls-eye) but running the numbers can give you a general idea of how your savings habits can impact your ability to generate long term wealth.

With that in mind, here are some basic assumptions for a hypothetical young person with a long time horizon ahead of them that you might see in a typical retirement calculator: Let's say you begin saving at age 25 with a target retirement age of 65. You begin saving 12% of your $40,000/year income that will grow by 3% per year.

So how much would our hypothetical retirement calculator saver end up with in this situation? Starting at an early age with a high savings rate would net more than $1.5 million by retirement.

Starting Age	25
Retirement Age	65
Annual Returns	7%
Annual Raise	3%
Starting Salary	$40,000
% of Income Saved	12%
Total Saved	$377,584
Ending Balance	$1,524,564
% from Saving	25%
% from Investing	75%

You can see that a steady diet of a double-digit savings rate coupled with decent investment returns and a healthy dose of compound interest can turn our hypothetical saver into a millionaire by the time they retire.

Looking at these numbers would lead you to believe that your investment returns carry the bulk of the load considering three-quarters of our saver's ending balance comes from compounded investment gains. But breaking out these results by different periods tells us a much different story.

Here's how things look by age 35 if you were to start saving at 25:

Age	35
Balance	$87,135
% from Saving	71%
% from Investing	29%

In the early years, the amount of money you put into your retirement account drives the bulk of your ending balance. Now here are the results by age 45:

Age	45
Balance	$274,932
% from Saving	50%
% from Investing	50%

It took more than 20 years for the investment gains to finally catch up to savings in terms of the contribution to the overall balance.

Here's a little secret about the compound interest that you cannot see in a retirement calculator - the majority of the growth comes once you build up a large enough balance as you get closer to retirement age. You can see this in action from the change in value over the final 10 years of saving and investing:

Balance at age 56	$739,559
Balance at age 65	$1,524,564

The gains from investing in the last 10 years in this example (age 56 to age 65) amount to $660,000, and more than 40% of the total ending balance.

This is where the Buffett example from the above comes into play. Obviously, it's a bit of an obnoxious comparison because the Oracle of Omaha is one of the richest people on the planet. But both Buffett's growth in assets and our retirement calculator example show how your money grows slowly until it builds upon itself and then explodes higher as compound interest takes off.

Real wealth for normal retirement savers comes from a combination of saving, compounding and sitting on your hands. It takes time and it's not easy. It could take decades to see extraordinary results, which is much longer than most people would prefer. Saving is more important than investing but saving is boring while investing is sexy. As life expectancy continues to increase, the virtue of patience and an understanding of your time horizon become more important than ever.

A few more lessons from this basic example:

- It's more exciting to focus on milking a few extra percentage points of investment returns out of the financial markets, but the amount you save in the first few decades of your career are far more important than your investment strategy.

- Increasing the savings rate on your income in this example from 12% to 15% has nearly the same effect on the ending balance as increasing investment performance by 1% per year. A savings rate of 20% instead of 12% equates to more than 2% a year in market returns. Earning higher returns on your investments is much more difficult than saving more money. You actually control your savings rate while no one controls what happens in the markets.

- Deconstructing compound interest into different time frames can help illustrate the power of sticking with a long term saving and investment plan. It may seem like every tick in the market is going to make or break your portfolio, when in reality the simple act of saving more money over the long-run can have an enormous impact on the size of your wealth.

- One study found nearly three-quarters of retirement success can be attributed to an individual's savings rate while the rest was explained by asset allocation and investment selections. For the majority of the population, saving is more important than investing.

It doesn't matter if you're the second coming of Warren Buffett if you don't save money. It takes money to compound money. Saving always comes before investing. But why should you save with the intent of investing in the first place?

The next chapter tackles this question.

CHAPTER 4.
WHY INVEST IN THE
FIRST PLACE?

The price of a movie ticket in 1970 was around one dollar and fifty cents. Today it's closer to ten dollars. That's a rise of more than 550% over 50 years which works out to an annual increase of nearly 4%. The average price of a new car in 1970 was $3,500 while the price for a gallon of gasoline was thirty-six cents. By 2020 those averages were close to $38,000 for a car and $2.20 for a gallon of gas, increases of 986% and 511%, respectively.

Saving is more important than investing when it comes to getting started with your finances. But if you ever hope to increase your standard of living, you have to grow your money over and above the rate of inflation. If you were to bury your money in your backyard, it would take just 23 years to see the value of your savings cut in half from a 3% annual inflation rate. At 4%, the half-life of your money would be just 17 years.

When Inflation Cuts Money in Half

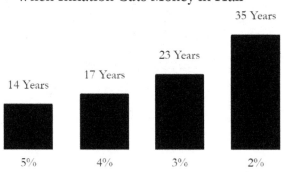

Inflation Rate

If you don't put your long term savings into productive financial assets, your money is going to lose its value. Let's look at one of the most popular shoe brands of all time to see why this is the case.

After being selected third overall by the Chicago Bulls in 1984 NBA Draft, Michael Jordan was signed to a five-year deal with Nike that was worth a reported $2.5 million, a hefty price tag at the time. A year later, Nike gave Jordan his own signature shoe. The Air Jordan was born.

The rest is history as Jordan went on to win six NBA titles, numerous MVP awards and become widely regarded as the best player to ever lace them up. There have since been over thirty different signature Air Jordan's in hundreds of different variations. Jordan's brand is so successful that he's now made far more money through his partnership with Nike than he ever made playing in the NBA. In 2019, the Jordan brand alone brought in more than $3 billion in revenue for Nike. That was good enough for roughly one-third of the total revenue for the entire company.

The first pair sold for $65, which was by far the most expensive basketball shoe on the market at the time. These shoes now regularly sell for $200 or more a pair while certain models can fetch thousands of dollars. It's now been well over thirty years since the first pair of Air Jordan's hit the market.

Three-plus decades is a substantial amount of time so I wanted to see what would have happened had you taken that $65 investment in a pair of Jordan's back in 1985 and matched it with a $65 investment in Nike (NKE) stock.

The price of Air Jordan grew from $65 in 1985 to $235 in 2019. That's an annual growth rate of 4% per year, outpacing the inflation rate of 2.5% over that time. But Nike's stock appreciated at a rate of more than 21% per year from 1985-2019. Had you invested $65 in the company in 1985, it would have been worth more than $36,000 by the end of 2019. That's an expensive pair of shoes.

This is an extreme example using one of the most successful companies in history but it illustrates the power of stock ownership over the long term and the need to invest in productive assets. The cost of stuff - houses, cars, food, clothing, etc. - generally goes up over time so you need to invest your money to protect your savings from the effects of inflation.

Time is your biggest enemy when it comes to the impact of inflation on your wealth. But time is also your biggest asset when it comes to growing your wealth.

A story about two different savers in the next chapter illustrates the importance of time as your biggest asset.

CHAPTER 5.
YOUR BIGGEST ASSET

Let's be honest - you and I probably can't spot the next Nike-like winner in the stock market. Here's a more realistic look at how even modest returns in the markets can lead to powerful results if you start early.

Sarah and Jon took two different paths on their retirement journey. Sarah was always a planner, so she made a point of saving once she found her first real job out of school. Jon, the other hand, opted out of saving right off the bat because he wanted to wait until he was ready later in life.

Sarah began saving for retirement at age 25, setting aside $500 a month in her workplace retirement account until age 35. At this point, she stopped saving and let compound interest work in her favor. At age 65, assuming a 7% annual rate of return she would retire with approximately $720,000 even though she only contributed a total of $66,000 to her account.

Jon put off his retirement savings for years because he couldn't bring himself around to the idea of investing in the stock market, which he assumed operated like a casino where the house always wins. Once he saw Sarah slowly building her wealth he finally decided to start saving at age 40. He followed her lead, saving the same $500 a month that Sarah did but he actually does so until the day he retires at age 65. The total amount Jon contributed to his retirement account over those two-plus decades would add up to $156,000. Assuming he also earns an annual return of 7% on his funds he will end up with around $412,000 when he retires.

Even though Jon contributed 2.5x as much money and saved for 2.5x as many years as Sarah, he ended up with $308,000 less than her at retirement. How could this be, you ask?

	Sarah	Jon
Started Saving	Age 25	Age 40
Stopped Saving	Age 35	Age 65
Total Saved	$66,000	$156,000
Ending Balance	$720,000	$412,000

Assumptions: Each saves $500/month and earns 7% on their investments

Sarah utilized her biggest asset - time - more favorably than Jon. Her savings compounded for a decade and a half longer, thus giving her money more time to snowball.

This is a simple example but let's not let Sarah off the hook that easily. There's no need to stop saving at age 35 just to prove a point about compound interest. Let's assume she doesn't stop saving at 35 but instead continues to dutifully sock away money each year until she reaches retirement age. Using these same inputs, she would now grow her portfolio to nearly $1.3 million by age 65. While Sarah would have saved $90,000 more in retirement contributions than Jon, she would have ended up with nearly $700,000 more by retirement age because she got an early start on saving.

The best thing you can do as a young person is to start saving and investing as soon as possible to take advantage of your long time horizon. According to financial writer William Bernstein:

Each dollar you do not save at 25 will mean two inflation-adjusted dollars that you will need to save if you start at age 35, four if you begin at 45, and eight if you start at 55. In practice, if you lack substantial savings at 45, you are in serious trouble. Since a 25-year-old should be saving at least 10 percent of his or her salary, this means that a 45-year-old will need to save nearly half of his or her salary.

Starting at a young age not only helps you take advantage of compound interest, it can save you stress and financial strain later in life. All is not lost if you're older and don't have access to a time machine but it will take some more planning and a higher savings rate (check out Chapter 22 for more on overcoming a late start to retirement saving).

I used $500 in this example because it's a nice, round number. But figuring out how much you need to save is one of the hardest questions to answer no matter where you are in relation to retirement age.

How much you should save is up next.

CHAPTER 6.
HOW MUCH SHOULD
YOU SAVE?

Offering financial advice is always tricky because so much of it is circumstantial. It's impossible to offer investment guidance if you don't know someone's goals, needs, desires, temperament, personality and current financial situation.

In lieu of knowing every reader's specific personal and financial circumstances, my only retirement rule of thumb is that **your savings rate should be in the double digits as a percentage of income**. If you do nothing else in your financial life than setting a high savings rate you'll be alright. Ten percent is a nice goal while 15% to 20% of your income would be even better. Can everyone afford to have a double-digit savings rate right off the bat? Of course not! But it's a goal you should work up to if you wish to create a large enough nest egg to reach financial independence someday.

There are a numerous benefits that accrue from introducing a double-digit savings rate in your life:

- It gives you a margin of safety when life interferes with your plans.
- It means you have less income to replace once you become financially independent.
- It reduces the many stresses that come as a result of money decisions.
- How much you spend is one of the few areas in life you have control over.

There are a few ways in which you can supercharge your savings to get to a double-digit savings rate over time even if it's not in the cards right away:

Treat it like a bill. We have a finite amount of willpower so trying to make it through your monthly budget and save whatever is leftover will eventually become a losing strategy. You have to make your savings automatic so you can't tinker with that decision. **Look at saving money like a monthly bill or subscription**, like paying for Netflix or a gym membership.

A 401(k) plan makes this easy and convenient because you set an amount or savings rate up front and don't ever even see the money hit your checking account since it's automatically routed to your retirement account. Once your saving is taken care of you don't need permission to spend elsewhere. You can spend money guilt-free without worry because your savings goals are taken care of. This is a way to think about budgeting in reverse.

Saving money should be prioritized every month just like rent/mortgage, utilities, Internet, streaming services and your car payment. The goal is to save enough money out of each paycheck that it hurts just a little bit.

Work your way up to it. Let's assume you want to start small because the prospect of saving lots of money from your paycheck is terrifying. If you save $100 a month towards retirement and your income is $60,000 a year, that's a savings rate of 2%. To get to our double-digit savings rate goal we have some work to do. Just a 1% increase in your savings rate every year could add hundreds of thousands of dollars to your portfolio over time.

Karen is 30 years old and makes sixty grand a year, saving $100 a month. If she were to simply keep saving 2% of her income (which grows at 3% per year for cost of living increases) every year until retiring at age 65, she would amass just shy of $260,000 assuming a 7% annual return on her investments.

Now let's see what happens if Karen were to increase her savings rate by just 1% per year. To hit a 15% savings rate goal it would take 14 years which sounds like forever. But this allows her to slowly grow into that savings rate. Using the same inputs as before, just a 1% increase for those 14 years and a flat 15% savings rate from then until retirement would grow her balance to $1.4 million. A 1% annual savings rate increase was worth more than $1 million over the life of

Karen's portfolio.

Most 401(k) plans allow you to automatically increase your savings rate over time as well to take this decision out of your own hands, which is the second most important step in your savings journey after just getting started. Most plans are now setting the default contribution at around 5% of income, so don't shy away from that if that's your starting point. Far too many retirement participants save a meager percentage of their income so setting future increases in motion ahead of time can keep you on track to avoid getting stuck at a low savings rate. A decent company match can help here as well.

Avoid lifestyle creep. The ability to witness your neighbor getting rich or buying stuff without getting jealous is a financial superpower. **Lifestyle creep is one of the biggest deterrents to saving money** because the more you make the more you feel you deserve. Making more money can make your life easier but you must ensure your spend rate doesn't outpace your savings if you ever wish to truly build wealth.

Let's go back to our 30 year old saver, Karen. She still makes $60,000 a year and saves 2% of her salary, which gets a 3% bump each year. Now let's assume she makes no other changes than saving half of her annual raise every year, thus allowing her to spend the remaining half to improve her standing in life. I call this the save-plus-reward strategy. Saving half of her raise each year would nearly double Karen's balance on her 2% savings rate from $256k to $433k.

Now let's take this one step further and see what would happen if Karen saved half of each raise AND increased her savings rate by 1% until it hit 15% by her mid-40s. Now by age 65 she has almost $1.6 million.

Starting small and slowly working your way up to your savings goal by avoiding lifestyle creep can provide a huge boost to your retirement savings.

Turbo charge your income. Saving money is important but cutting back on your spending can only take you so far in life financially.

Most financial experts preach the virtues of frugality to get ahead but earning more money is how you supercharge your savings. **The best investment you'll ever make is in yourself.** Negotiating a $10,000 raise early in your career could be worth close to $1,000,000 over the course of your career. Here are three different scenarios that show what this single raise could turn into if you prioritize it in terms of saving:

	Save 25% of Annual Raise	Save 50% of Annual Raise	Save 75% of Annual Raise
After 10 Years	$33,982	$67,965	$101,947
After 20 Years	$112,368	$224,737	$337,105
After 30 Years	$292,934	$585,867	$878,801

Assumptions: 6% annual return and 3% raise each year on a $10k initial raise in salary

Now think about how much of an impact a few raises over the course of your career could have on your wealth if you approach them in this manner. You have to make a concerted effort to save any additional income but the hard part for most people is actually earning more money. If you're stuck career-wise I've always loved Theo Epstein's 20% rule for getting ahead. The Red Sox and Cubs savior once told David Axelrod:

Whoever your boss is, or your bosses are, they have 20 percent of their job that they just don't like. So if you can ask them or figure out what that 20 percent is, and figure out a way to do it for them, you'll make them really happy, improve their quality of life and their work experience.

You also must become comfortable negotiating, having uncomfortable conversations and building a network of people who will look out for your career prospects. If you can't sell yourself you'll have little chance of making more money.

Once you figure out how to get to that goal of a double-digit savings rate you need to figure out where to put that money.

CHAPTER 7.
WHAT TO INVEST IN

Let's say you want to start a new business - the Uber of peanut butter and jelly sandwiches. You know, when people need a PB&J stat because they're so hungry they need it delivered ASAP. You think it's the next big tech company but you don't have enough money to start your dream business.

You have two options to get PB & Juber off the ground. Option one is to borrow money from a bank through a small business loan where you pay back the principal over time with interest. Option two, is selling equity in the business to family, friends or outside investors where they are entitled to a portion of the profits and/or the proceeds if the business is sold or goes public.

There are pros and cons to each funding option. If your PB&J business does wonderfully, there is huge potential upside for anyone who purchased an ownership stake to earn higher profits or see the value of their ownership stake increase. A lender, on the other hand, is only going to make the agreed upon interest income payment and get their principal repayment when the loan comes due.

If your PB&J business does terribly, there is huge potential downside for anyone who purchased an ownership stake to see lower profits and the value of their ownership stake fall or even going to zero in the worst case scenario. A lender, on the other hand, is legally obligated to their debt repayments and would be first in line for any payments or asset forfeitures before the stockholders in the event of a bankruptcy if people decide PB&J on demand isn't something they're interested in.

Financial assets have a similar risk profile. Investing in stocks offers big potential upside but it comes at the risk of big downside potential. Owning high-quality debt or bonds lowers the risk of large losses but that protection is offset by the fact that your upside potential is capped. Cash flows paid to the owners of stocks are also far more volatile than those for bondholders because corporations have their own unique business risks and can get into trouble if the economy struggles

There is no right or wrong answer in terms of how you deploy your capital between being an owner (stocks) and being a lender (bonds). But, how you allocate your retirement dollars between the two is one of the most important decisions you will make as an investor because it sets the tone for your portfolio's risk profile.

If you only understand one concept about the risk of investing your capital let it be this: You cannot earn high returns on your money over the long-run without accepting losses or bone-crushing volatility at times. And you cannot keep your money safe from losses and bone-crushing volatility over the short-run if you're not willing to accept lower returns over the long-run. **Risk never goes away completely, it just gets transferred somewhere else.** This is the essence of risk and reward when investing your savings.

Understanding risk and reward in the stock market is on deck.

CHAPTER 8.
HOW THE STOCK
MARKET WORKS

After getting engaged my wife and I began having some deeper philosophical conversations about how we would run our joint finances. We were in our mid-to-late 20s at the time so I informed her I would like to put the majority of our retirement savings into the stock market.

This was obviously a topic initiated by yours truly since I am the personal finance nerd of the relationship but she was all for it. We covered our spending habits, budgeting, saving, debt, bill payments and how we generally planned on setting long term financial goals. It was a great talk and one I recommend every couple have at some point if they plan on staying together for the long haul. The fastest way to lose half of your money is not a stock market crash but a divorce so it's a good idea to make sure you're on the same page when it comes to your finances.

Since we both come from similar backgrounds when in terms of saving, spending, credit card debt and living below our means this was a pretty easy conversation considering how problematic finances can be for some couples. But there was one area where my wife needed some more clarity. And that was the topic of investing our retirement savings in the stock market.

My wife, like most normal people, did not know much about the stock market except for what she heard on the news or saw on TV and in the movies. She did not give much thought to investing in stocks. So when I told her we would be saving the bulk of our retirement money in stocks (especially when we were younger) she was initially concerned.

Aren't stocks extremely risky?

Isn't this just gambling with our money?

Isn't there a chance we could lose most of our money?

Shouldn't we just play it safe?

Working in the finance industry, I'm no stranger to an Excel spreadsheet or PowerPoint presentation but I needed to put this explainer into plain English to avoid boring her and get my point across. What follows is more or less what I told her (and despite going through this exercise she still agreed to marry me if you can believe it).

The stock market is the only place where anyone can invest in human ingenuity. It is a bet on the future being better than today. Stocks can be thought of as a way to ride the coattails of intelligent people and businesses as they continue to innovate and grow. Short of owning your own business, buying shares in the stock market is the simplest way to own a slice of the business world.

The greatest part about owning shares in the stock market is you can earn money by doing nothing more than holding onto them. When companies pay out dividends to shareholders, you get cold hard cash sent to your brokerage or retirement account which you can choose to either reinvest or spend as you please. The stock market is one of the few places on earth where you can earn passive income without having to do any work whatsoever. All you have to do is buy and wait. And if global stock markets don't go up over the long term you'll have bigger problems on your hands than your 401(k) balance.

Many people compare the stock market to a casino but in a casino the odds are stacked against you. The longer you play in a casino, the greater the odds you'll walk away a loser because the house wins based on pure probability. It's just the opposite in the stock market.

The longer your time horizon, historically, the better your odds are at seeing positive outcomes. Now these positive outcomes don't guarantee a specific rate of return, even over longer time frames. If the stock market were consistent in the returns it spits out, there would be no risk.

S&P 500: 1926-2020

Time Frame	Positive	Negative
Daily	56%	44%
1 Year	75%	25%
5 Years	88%	12%
10 Years	95%	5%
20 Years	100%	0%

Source: Dimensional Fund Advisors

If there were no risk, there would be no wonderful long term returns. And because there is risk involved when owning stocks, your returns can vary widely depending on when you invest in the stock market.

S&P 500 Annual Returns: 1926-2020

	5 Years	10 Years	20 Years	30 Years
Best	36.1%	21.4%	18.3%	14.8%
Worst	-17.4%	-4.9%	1.9%	7.8%
Average	10.1%	10.4%	10.9%	11.2%

Source: Dimensional Fund Advisors

It has been possible to lose money over decade-long periods in the past. Even 20 to 30 year results can see a big spread between the best and worst outcomes. However, it is worth noting that even the worst annual returns over 30 years in the history of the U.S. stock market would have produced a total return of more than 850%. This is the beauty of compounding. The *worst* 30 year return for the S&P 500 gave you more than 8x your initial investment.

The stock market is a compounding machine in other ways as well. Since 1950, the largest companies in the U.S. stock market have seen dividends paid out per share grow from roughly $1 to $60 by 2020.

Profits have grown from $2 a share to $100 a share. Those are growth rates of roughly 6000% and 5000%, respectively, over the past 70 years or so, good enough for 6% annual growth for each. One dollar invested in the U.S. stock market in 1950 would be worth more than $2,000 by the end of 2020.

$10,000 dollars invested in the S&P 500 in the year:

- 2010 would be worth $37,600 by September 2020

- 2000 would be worth $34,200 by September 2020

- 1990 would be worth $182,300 by September 2020

- 1980 would be worth $918,500 by September 2020

- 1970 would be worth $1,623,500 by September 2020

- 1960 would be worth $3,445,000 by September 2020

I'm ignoring the effects of fees, taxes, trading costs, etc. here but the point remains that over the long haul, the stock market is unrivaled when it comes to growing money. And the longer you're in it the better your chances of compounding.

Having said all of that, there is an unfortunate side-effect of this long term compounding machine. Stocks can rip your heart out over the short term. **If there is an ironclad rule in the world of investing, it's that risk and reward are always and forever attached at the hip**. You can't expect to earn outsized gains if you don't expose yourself to the possibility of outsized losses. The reason that stocks earn higher returns than bonds or cash over time is because there will be periods of excruciating losses.

That $1 invested in 1950 would grow to $17 by the end of 1972 and subsequently drop to $10 by fall of 1974. From there it would grow to $95 by the fall of 1987, only to drop to $62 over the course of a single week because of the Black Monday crash. That $62 would have turned into an unbelievable $604 by spring of 2000. By the fall of 2002 that $604 would have been down to just $340. After slowly working its way all the way to $708 by the fall of 2007, over the next year-and-a-half it would be cut in half down to $347 by March 2009. By the end of December 2009 that initial $1 was worth $537, which is less than the $590 it was worth a decade earlier by the end of 1999. So $1 growing turning into $2,000 sounds amazing until you realize the many fluctuations it took to get there. The stock market goes up a lot over the long term because sometimes it can go down by a lot over the short term.

The stock market is fueled by differences in opinions, goals, time horizons and personalities over the short term and fundamentals over the long term. At times this means stocks overshoot to the upside and go higher than fundamentals would dictate. Other times stocks overshoot to the downside and go lower than fundamentals would dictate. The biggest reason for this is because people can lose their minds when they come together as a group. As long as markets are made up of human decisions it will always be like this. Think about how crazy fans can get when their team wins, loses or gets screwed over by the refs. These same emotions are at work when money is involved.

How you feel about investing in the stock market should have more to do with your place in the investor's lifecycle than your feelings about volatility.

Now let's look at the importance of lifecycle investing.

CHAPTER 9.
THE INVESTOR'S
LIFECYCLE

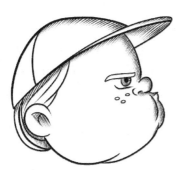

As I write this book, I'm entering the last year of my 30s. Please respect my privacy as I go through the mourning process before turning 40. According to the Social Security actuary table, people my age live to be 79 years old, on average. Let's keep things optimistic and say I'm above average in terms of longevity. I have somewhere in the order of four or more decades remaining to prepare for financially over the rest of my life.

In the coming 40-50 years I'm planning on experiencing at least 10 or more bear markets, including 5 or 6 that constitute a market crash in stocks. There will also probably be at least 7-8 recessions in that time as well, maybe more.

Can I be sure of these numbers? You can never be sure of anything when it comes to the markets or economy but let's use history as a rough guide on this. Over the 50 years from 1970-2019, there were 7 recessions, 10 bear markets and 4 legitimate market crashes with losses in excess of 30% for the U.S. stock market. Over the previous 50 years from 1920-1969, there were 11 recessions, 15 bear markets, and 8 legitimate market crashes with losses in excess of 30% for the U.S. stock market.

Bear markets, brutal market crashes and recessions are a fact of life as an investor. They are a feature, not a bug of the system in which we save and invest our money. So you may as well get used to dealing with them because they're not going away anytime soon. They can't because the markets and economy are run by humans and humans always take everything, both good times and bad, too far.

The risk of these crashes and economic downturns is not the same for everyone though. How you view the inevitable setbacks when dealing with your life savings has more to do with your station in life than how scary you think those times are. **Risk means different**

things to different people depending on where they reside in the investor's lifecycle.

When you're young, human capital (or lifetime earning potential) is a far greater asset than your investment capital. If you're in your 20s, 30s or even 40s you still have many years ahead of you as a net saver and earner, meaning market volatility should be welcomed, not feared. Down markets lead to higher dividend yields, lower valuations and more opportunities to buy stocks at lower price points. It may not feel like it at the time but if you're saving money periodically this is a good thing.

There's an old saying that the stock market is the only business where the product goes on sale and all of the customers run out of the store. **Your actions during down markets have larger say in your success or failure as an investor than how you act during rising markets.** The problem is during a market crash, it will always feel like it's too late to sell but too early to buy. If time is on your side, you shouldn't worry about nailing the timing on your retirement contributions, especially during down markets. The good thing about being a young person is you don't need to worry about timing the market to succeed. You have the ability to wait out bear markets since you have such a long runway in front of you.

Retirees, on the other hand, are lacking in human capital but (hopefully) sitting on plenty of financial capital. People are living longer, meaning the management of your money isn't over when you retire. But you have to be more thoughtful about how your life savings is invested in retirement because you don't have nearly as much time to wait out a down market, nor do you have the earning power to deploy new savings when stocks are down by buying when there's blood in the streets.

Market risk not only has different connotations depending on where you are in the investor's lifecycle, but also how you're wired personality-wise. Your risk profile as an investor is determined by some combination of your ability, willingness and need to take risk. These three forces are rarely in a state of equilibrium so there will always have to be some trade-offs.

Your **ability to take risk** involves your time horizon, liquidity constraints, income profile and financial resources.

Your **willingness to take risk** involves your risk appetite. It's the difference between your desire to grow your wealth and your desire to protect your wealth.

Your **need to take risk** involves determining the required rate of return necessary to reach your goals.

Those who are unprepared for retirement may need to take more risk in their portfolio to achieve their goals but they may not have the willingness or ability.

Those who have more than enough money saved may have the ability and willingness to take more risk to grow their wealth but they may not need to because they have already won the game.

Rarely do the planets align when it comes to figuring out the right investment mix but the good news is there is no such thing as the perfect portfolio. The perfect portfolio only exists with the benefit of hindsight. And even if the perfect investment strategy did exist it would be useless if you couldn't stick with it over the long term. A half-decent investment strategy you can stick with is vastly superior to an extraordinary investment strategy you can't stick with. Discipline and a long time horizon are the big equalizers when it comes to financial success.

Your ability to withstand losses in the market and stay the course with your plan come hell or high water comes down to some combination of time horizon, risk profile, human capital, temperament and ego. If you don't understand yourself, your circumstances and your deficiencies when making decisions about money, it's impossible to truly gauge your tolerance for risk.

Now let me tell you why picking stocks is harder than you think.

CHAPTER 10.
PICKING STOCKS IS
HARDER THAN
YOU THINK

General Electric was the largest company in the U.S. stock market in the year 2000. Not only was it the biggest company in the market but it was nearly double the size of the second largest corporation, Exxon. From the start of the new century in 2000 through the fall of 2020, GE shares were down 80% and that includes the reinvestment of all dividends. Retirees who kept the bulk of their retirement assets in the stock are in a world of pain. Nearly one third of GE's 401(k) plan were invested in company shares as recently as 2016.

And this is just a once great stock that had a fall from grace. Employees who had their retirement money in the stock of Enron or Lehman Brothers or WorldCom lost everything when these companies went under.

According to researcher Geoffrey West, GE, Enron, Lehman and WorldCom are not alone. It's very difficult to sustain a corporation over the long term:

- Nearly 29,000 companies traded on the U.S. stock market from 1950-2009. Almost 80% were gone by 2009 (through buyouts, mergers, bankruptcy, etc.)

- Fewer than 5% of companies in the stock market remain over rolling 30 year periods.

- The risk of a company dying did not depend on its age or size. The probability of a 5-year-old company dying before it turns 6 is the same as that of a 50-year-old company reaching age 51.

- The estimated half-life of U.S. publicly traded companies was 10.5, meaning half of all companies that go public in any given year will be gone in 10.5 years.

- There was just a 12% survival rate for the firms that were on the Fortune 500 list in 1955.

Forget outperforming the market; simply surviving as a corporation is hard enough over the long term.

What do you think about this stock? Should I buy it?

This is probably the question I've been asked more than any other from people who know I work in the finance industry. There is typically a look of befuddlement on their faces when I politely decline to offer guidance with my standard "I don't know."

And the truth is I really don't know. Picking stocks is ridiculously hard. One of the secrets to investing is stock-picking isn't nearly as important as people on financial television would have you believe. Here's a shortlist of things that are more important than stock-picking:

- **Your savings rate.** Saving is the first step to investing.

- **Your asset allocation.** The mix of stocks, bonds, cash and other investments will be the biggest determinant of your investment success beyond how much you save because it sets the tone for the risk profile of your portfolio.

- **Your investment plan.** Financial writer Nick Murray says, "A portfolio is not, in and of itself, a plan. And a portfolio that isn't in service to a plan is just a form of speculation; it can have no other goal than to beat most other people's portfolios. But "outperformance" isn't a financial goal."

If a portfolio isn't a plan then neither is stock-picking. I'll admit, picking stocks is more fun than asset allocation but it's also much harder to pull off. For every Amazon that turns a small initial investment into millions of dollars, there are thousands of companies that would decimate your life savings.

An eye-opening study from JP Morgan found roughly 40% of all stocks in the U.S. stock market have suffered a permanent 70%+ decline from their peak value since 1980. Two-thirds of all stocks underperformed the stock market itself in that time while 40% of companies experienced negative returns. There have, of course, been some big winners in this time but it is a select group of stocks. Around 7% of companies in the U.S. stock market have generated lifetime returns that would make them fall into the category of "extreme winners." According to Hendrik Bessembinder's research, **4 out of every 7 stocks in the United States has underperformed the return of cash sitting in a savings account since 1926.** There are simply more opportunities to pick the losers than the winners in the stock market.

Diversifying your investments among a large number of stocks means you won't hit home runs but it also takes striking out off the table. The key to diversification is that you don't need to select the winners in advance. The cream rises to the top automatically. Normal investors should be happy to accept singles and doubles since it means you're not at risk of one or two bad investments destroying your life savings.

Companies can go to zero. Target date funds and index funds do not.

CHAPTER 11.
THE ONE-STOP SHOP
RETIREMENT FUND

Every year I get asked to participate in a fantasy football league with my friends, neighbors or co-workers. And each year I politely decline. For some reason I just never got into it and don't have the time, energy or motivation to figure it out now (I'm also a Detroit Lions fan so I already have enough anxiety surrounding the NFL). Nothing against those who are into made-up football teams but it's just not for me.

My feelings about fantasy football are how many people feel about managing their investments. They simply don't care enough to learn how to do it or they have other things they would rather spend their time on. Personally, I love working through the intricacies of portfolio management, asset allocation and investment strategy. But I understand the do-it-yourself approach is not for everyone. Many people's eyes glaze over when thinking about mutual funds, ETFs, diversification and choosing the right mix of asset classes.

And there's nothing wrong with this line of thinking. It all depends on how much control you would like over the process. If you're like me and find this stuff intellectually stimulating, you can always pick your own asset allocation, choose the funds or securities within those asset classes and manually shift your asset class mix over time as your risk profile or circumstances change.

Or you could go the easy route and simply pick a target date fund in your 401(k), IRA or brokerage account. Target date funds are one of the best developments for individual investors in decades because they take many of the investment decisions out of your hands and automate the process for you. It's a huge step forward for normal investors who don't have the bandwidth to do this themselves.

The main reason target date funds are so important to retirement savers is because of a rule change in the Pension Reform Act of 2006 which requires workplace retirement plans to provide a legitimate default investment option for their employees who sign up. In the past, most of these plans would default to a conservative fixed income or stable value fund. Most people don't know how to pick their own funds or rarely make changes to their investment options, so this made it difficult for people to know where to begin when they started saving.

So how do they work?

Each target date fund has a literal date in its name that signifies when you would be retiring. So let's assume you're 35 years old and plan to retire at age 65. If you started investing in the year 2020, a target date 2050 fund would line up with your time horizon since the retirement date on that fund is 30 years away. These all-in-one funds invest across asset classes (stocks and bonds) and geographies (U.S. and foreign stocks and bonds) to give you a well-diversified portfolio. The investment company that manages the fund chooses the asset allocation based on your age, shifting from a stock-heavy portfolio in your younger years into a more balanced allocation as you near retirement. This change to the portfolio mix is called the glidepath because it's a gradual shift over time. They will also automatically rebalance the fund for you back to the stated asset class target weights over time.

Target date holdings can vary by fund company but if you want to take more or less risk depending on your appetite for stocks, you can always choose a fund with a different retirement date. For instance, let's assume Patrick is 25 but is still unsure of his ability to deal with losses in the stock market. Instead of going with a target date 2060 fund he could pick the 2050 or 2045 option which would have a lower allocation to stocks. Or how about Paula, who is 45 but plans on working well into her 70s and is willing to accept more stock market risk. Instead of going with the 2040 target date fund, she could pick the 2050 or 2055 fund to hold more stocks.

Most retirement plan sponsors elect a target date fund as the default investment choice when they set up a 401(k) plan. This is a powerful behavior nudge and one that has led to an explosion in the popularity of these funds. Close to 80% of 401(k) investors now hold a target date fund in the retirement plans sponsored by fund giant Vanguard.

Target date funds aren't perfect. You can't customize the holdings to suit your exact needs or asset allocation preferences. There's no one there to hold your hand or explain exactly how these funds work (retirement advice varies by plan sponsor and is often severely lacking). The allocations and glide paths can vary depending on the fund company. As with all investment strategies you could always do better, but it's also much easier to do worse than a target date fund. If nothing else, they are a great way for investors who are just starting out to gain exposure to a broadly diversified portfolio without having to figure out the specific holdings themselves.

If you would like some more customization to your specific goals, risk profile and time horizon beyond a target date fund, you can always sign up with a robo-advisor outside of a workplace retirement plan using an IRA or taxable account. Robo-advisors will create a portfolio just for you that suits your various needs and goals. Perhaps the best feature of these services is the fact that the saving and investing is automated for you after you sign up and fill out some general information about your circumstances.

The beauty of an all-in-one fund structure or automated solution is that it cuts down on the temptation to tinker with your portfolio. Target date funds or robo-advisors can reduce the temptation to make poor investment decisions at the worst possible time. These funds and services are designed to protect you from your worst impulses as an investor.

When choosing the right fund or funds for your retirement account, there is one variable that matters more than any other.

That variable can be explained through a story about my brother's first car and how it cost my father his New Year's resolution.

CHAPTER 12.
YOU GET WHAT YOU
DON'T PAY FOR

When I was in high school my dad told everyone in the family his New Year's resolution was to avoid swearing. My father is a pretty laid back guy but everyone has a breaking point that causes them to drop a four-letter word. That breaking point came in the form of an Isuzu Trooper. When my older brother turned 16, my parents bought him the Trooper for his first vehicle. An SUV seemed like an intelligent choice to navigate the brutal winters of Northern Michigan. Unfortunately, this particular SUV was a piece of junk that was constantly breaking down and in need of repairs.

One January evening I was getting dropped off by some friends in the middle of a snowstorm and noticed my mother, father and brother were all outside trying to figure out what was wrong with the Trooper this time. The only thing I could make out when stepping onto the driveway was my mom admonishing my dad with, "Eddie! There goes your New Year's resolution!" as my dad swore up a storm at my brother's lemon of a car. They likely ended up spending more on repairs than the car itself.

The whole family learned a valuable lesson from this experience - there are certain things in life where you get what you pay for. A good steak. A high quality washer and dryer. A nice pair of shoes. The right mattress. A quality car that won't constantly break down on you. You get what you pay for when it comes to stuff like this.

For investors, the opposite is true. As the late-Jack Bogle often reminded investors, you get what you *don't* pay for. The Vanguard founder's core investing principle rested on the Cost Matters Hypothesis:

> *The case for indexing isn't based on the efficient market hypothesis. It's based on the simple arithmetic of the cost matters hypothesis. In many areas of the market, there will be a loser for every winner so, on average, investors*

will get the return of that market less fees.

Index funds are hard to beat because you get to keep more of the returns by paying lower fees than investors pay in actively managed funds. Not only are the expenses lower on these funds, thus offering you a larger percentage of the take home return, but they trade less, meaning there are fewer transaction costs. This is the exact opposite of most things you buy in other areas of your life, which is one of the reasons investing can be so counterintuitive.

Investment research firm Morningstar performed a study that looked at all of the variables that predicted the future success or failure of a mutual fund in terms of its performance. The variable with the higher predictive power had nothing to do with the intelligence of the portfolio manager selecting the stocks or their ability to forecast the future or which Ivy League university they attended. The variable with the most predictive power was cost. Looking across every asset class, Morningstar found the cheapest 20% of funds were 3 times as likely to succeed as the most expensive 20% of funds. **When it comes to investing, being cheap is a virtue.**

If you based your investment decisions on nothing else other than choosing the funds with the lowest costs, you would likely do better than 70-80% of all investors. All else equal, if you're choosing a mutual fund or ETF in your 401(k), 403(b), Roth IRA or brokerage account, picking the one with the lowest cost is a good starting point. And if you're picking a target date fund, try to find the one that holds mostly index funds. Holding low-cost funds doesn't guarantee that you'll earn higher returns on your savings but it does guarantee you'll take home more on a net basis than the alternative the majority of the time.

Compound interest can provide a tailwind over the long-haul when it comes to growing your wealth but fund fees can quietly counteract this advantage if you're not careful. To be fair, there are certainly higher cost, more actively managed funds that have delivered superior returns for their investors after fees. If these funds are able to deliver a smoother ride that allows you to stay invested over the long haul that's a win from a behavioral perspective. The best strategy is the one you can stick with through thick and thin. Regardless of what you invest in, it's best to make sure you know what you own and why you own it to ensure your expectations are aligned with your portfolio.

Of course, expense ratios are not the only costs you incur as an investor. The biggest cost can often come from your own behavior in terms of constantly trying to time the market by jumping in and out of your investments depending on how you feel about the current market or economic environment. Your biggest enemies when it comes to investing are inflation, taxes, costs and human nature.

One of the simplest ways to avoid the siren song of market timing is to diversify your investments across time.

Volatility and dollar cost averaging are the next topic.

CHAPTER 13.
DIVERSIFYING ACROSS TIME

One of the biggest benefits the advent of target date funds has provided individual investors is the ability to diversify their investments in a simple, cost-effective manner using a single fund. But there is another simple way to diversify your retirement assets that has nothing to do with the investments you choose.

Murphy's Law states anything that can go wrong will go wrong. Investors often feel this way about the timing of their purchases into the stock market. There's always a nagging worry that you'll invest your money right before a huge crash. The beauty of being a long term retirement saver is that your purchases are spread out over a wide range of market environments.

The majority of normal investors aren't investing on day one with a huge pool of capital unless they have uber-rich parents or a large inheritance. Instead, you're investing money periodically out of your paycheck or making contributions on a set schedule from your bank account, slowly but surely building your wealth.

This dollar cost averaging is diversifying across time because sometimes you're buying when the market is screaming higher, sometimes you're buying when markets are getting crushed and sometimes you're buying when markets are somewhere in-between. If you're investing consistently like this, it means sometimes you'll buy more shares with the same amount of money (when markets are falling) and sometimes you'll buy fewer shares with the same amount of money (when markets are rising).

The most important aspect of this strategy is that you simply keep buying no matter what. Trying to get too cute with the timing of your purchases is sure to lead to suboptimal results eventually because market timing is a game no one can win consistently. This is true even if you try to create a strategy where you only buy when markets are down, which seems counterintuitive to the oldest investment advice in the world - buy low and sell high.

Financial writer Nick Maggiulli performed a study to test this theory by comparing two buying strategies - one simple and one God-like. The first strategy would invest $100 (adjusted for inflation) into the U.S. stock market every month for 40 years. We'll call this the simple approach to investing. The God-like strategy was completely unrealistic but it assumes you only put that $100 dollars to work at the absolute low point between two all-time highs in the market. So this isn't just a buy low strategy, but a buy at the bottom of the market in every cycle.

So which approach was the winner?

Shockingly, the simple approach beat God, scoring a 70% win rate going all the way back to the 1920s. And missing the exact bottom of the market in the God-like strategy would take the win rate for that strategy from 30% to just 3%. Plus, no one is good enough to buy at or near the bottom of every bear market. This is the tortoise beating the hare even when the hare has Usain Bolt's speed. Maggiulli concludes, "Even God couldn't beat dollar cost averaging."

The reason the simple approach beats God is because investing on a regular basis over the long haul gives your savings more time to grow. Constantly trying to invest at the bottom of the market means sitting on the sidelines and missing out on valuable dividend payments and market appreciation. And since the stock market, over time, goes up more often than it goes down, you could be waiting a long time for a better entry point if you try to time your purchases.

When dollar cost averaging sometimes you buy higher. Sometimes you buy lower. Sometimes you buy when stocks are undervalued. Sometimes you buy when stocks are overvalued. The only thing that matters is that you keep buying. You're not beholden to any single point in time. When viewed from this perspective, volatility in the stock market is no longer your enemy but your friend. It allows you to average in at different price points during different market environments. As a net saver, you should welcome down markets from time to time. Young people with decades ahead of them should say a prayer for falling markets every night before they go to bed.

The only thing that matters is that you keep buying. Fortunately, for 401(k) participants, this is already happening with contributions you make each pay period.

This is especially true when stocks go down.

CHAPTER 14.
YOU WILL LOSE MONEY

Only three things in life are promised – death, taxes and stock market declines. The U.S. stock market has experienced double-digit losses in more than half of all years since 1950. Nine out of every 10 years has seen losses of at least 5% at some point during the year. It's perfectly normal for markets to freak out on a periodic basis, because humans freak out from time to time as reality does not always line up with expectations.

As an investor in the stock market, you have to get used to existing in a state of loss because the market is below all-time highs the majority of the time. Since 1928, the S&P 500 has hit new all-time highs in roughly 5% of all trading sessions. If we invert this number, that means 95% of the time investors are in a state of drawdown and stocks are down from a previous high watermark.

In the short term, the reasons for market sell-offs feel like they matter a lot and downturns feel like they'll never end. In the long term, investors tend to forget the specific reasons stocks fell in the past and all corrections look like buying opportunities.

Another benefit of making periodic contributions to your retirement account is the psychological boost they can provide in the midst of a downturn. This is especially true for those just starting out on their retirement savings journey without a sizable portfolio just yet.

An investor who doesn't have a lot of money set aside should be able to withstand larger percentage losses because the actual dollar decline will be relatively small. On the other hand, an investor with a lot of money in their portfolio can see a relatively small percentage loss lead to a much bigger loss of dollars. For example, these are the dollar losses based on different portfolio sizes and percentage losses:

Loss	$10,000	$50,000	$100,000	$250,000	$500,000	$1,000,000
-10%	-$1,000	-$5,000	-$10,000	-$25,000	-$50,000	-$100,000
-20%	-$2,000	-$10,000	-$20,000	-$50,000	-$100,000	-$200,000
-30%	-$3,000	-$15,000	-$30,000	-$75,000	-$150,000	-$300,000
-40%	-$4,000	-$20,000	-$40,000	-$100,000	-$200,000	-$400,000
-50%	-$5,000	-$25,000	-$50,000	-$125,000	-$250,000	-$500,000

As Captain Obvious likes to say, "the bigger your portfolio the more money you lose for a given percentage decline." This works in both directions as the inverse of these losses would show greater dollar gains with larger portfolio balances as well.

When you have a small portfolio that you're looking to make into a big portfolio, you have the ability to make up for short term losses by increasing your savings rate. We can call this your savings replacement rate. Let's assume you have the ability max out your IRA (the contribution limit for an IRA in 2020 is $6,000). These are the savings replacement rates for various loss levels based on making the max IRA contribution each year:

Losses covered if you max out your IRA ($6,500)

Loss	$10,000	$50,000	$100,000	$250,000	$500,000	$1,000,000
-10%	600%	120%	60%	24%	12%	6%
-20%	300%	60%	30%	12%	6%	3%
-30%	200%	40%	20%	8%	4%	2%
-40%	150%	30%	15%	6%	3%	2%
-50%	120%	24%	12%	5%	2%	1%

A 20% downturn on a $25,000 portfolio would lead to losses of $5,000. It's never fun to see that money temporarily disappear but maxing out your IRA would more than make up for the market value loss in your portfolio and leave you with an ending balance of $26,000 in that scenario.

Captain Obvious here again - making retirement contributions doesn't improve your actual performance but it could help you stay the course during a market downturn if you're still able to see some progres. Here are those same results if you maxed it out your 401(k) which had a max contribution limit of $19,500 in 2020:

Losses covered if you max out your 401(k) ($19,500)

Loss	$10,000	$50,000	$100,000	$250,000	$500,000	$1,000,000
-10%	1950%	390%	195%	78%	39%	20%
-20%	975%	195%	98%	39%	20%	10%
-30%	650%	130%	65%	26%	13%	7%
-40%	488%	98%	49%	20%	10%	5%
-50%	390%	78%	39%	16%	8%	4%

If you have $250,000 saved in your 401(k), a 20% loss would mean $50,000 evaporated for the time being. That stings but maxing out your 401(k) would be the equivalent of roughly 40% of those losses (and I'm not even including a company match here). It's also worth pointing out losses in the overall stock market aren't permanent. The only permanent losses during a panic come when you sell.

This line of thinking is more about optics than anything but psychological tricks can come in handy during down markets because behavior is the first thing to go during stressful market situations. **Sometimes you have to fool yourself into staying the course because the temptation to sell is so great when prices are all over the map.**

Tricking yourself into saving more can be more useful than most people imagine because knowledge alone is never enough to change your behavior.

CHAPTER 15. WHEN INFORMATION IS USELESS

Consider the following statistics from the CDC:

- In the 1960s just over 13% of Americans qualified as obese.

- By the 1970s this number was closer to 15%.

- Obesity numbers exploded in the 1980s and 1990s as more than 30% of people were considered obese.

- Today more than two-thirds of Americans are either overweight or obese.

- Obesity is the second leading cause of preventable death, after smoking.

The biggest head-scratcher of these numbers is the fact that the diet and exercise craze really took off for the first time starting in the 1960s. People spend more money on this stuff than ever before yet the results are going in the wrong direction. Between 1989 and 2012, Americans collectively spent more than $1 trillion dollars on weight loss solutions. What did they have to show for this investment? Obesity in the United States grew by more than 50% while extreme obesity doubled. Diets, exercise techniques, gyms and workout gurus are more plentiful now than at any time in history yet people in this country continue to get unhealthier by the year. More than $1 trillion dollars was thrown at a growing problem over almost 25 years and things only got worse.

Human nature is such a powerful force that it can act against your own best interests. **Knowledge alone is never enough to change behavior**. Just look at the scary retirement statistics I shared in the introduction to this book. It's impossible to read numbers like that without grimacing and shaking your head. But do scary retirement statistics get people to change their behavior? Of course not!

Statistics don't stick with us but stories do. Most people prefer get rich quick schemes to thoughtful advice on how to get rich slowly for the same reason people seek out fad diets. Tactics are easier to latch onto than wholesale lifestyle changes because they make you feel like you're accomplishing something. This is the opposite of the power of small wins. It's the acceleration of small losses.

It is a cliche at this point to compare personal finance to dieting and fitness but this is as good of an explanation as any as to why financial literacy fails to help people improve their money skills. The solutions for both personal finance and getting healthy are fairly simple in theory:

- For your finances: Spend less than you earn, live below your means, prioritize your spending, save and invest early and often and don't take on excessive levels of debt.

- For your health: Exercise regularly, don't overindulge, avoid too much sugar and carbs, eat less, and plan out your eating habits in advance.

Unfortunately, this **information is useless unless it's paired with a concrete plan to change behavior.** It's estimated that 95% of people who lose weight using a diet end up gaining the weight back. Bad habits are hard to break.

Food researcher Brian Wansink once wrote, "The best diet is the one you don't know you're on."

This is a wonderful way to think about implementing a workable saving and budgeting plan as well.

Automating your saving and spending is up next.

CHAPTER 16.
TREAT YOUR SAVINGS
LIKE A NETFLIX
SUBSCRIPTION

Cartoonist Randy Glasbergen drew a single frame comic that perfectly encapsulates the conflict that occupies nearly every financial decision you make in life. The cartoon depicts a man sitting in his financial advisor's office saying "Explain to me again why enjoying life when I retire is more important than enjoying life now."

This is deep.

This inner struggle can be taken to both extremes. There are those people who save nothing, live paycheck-to-paycheck and never plan ahead for their future financial well-being. And then there are those people who are frugal to a fault and never spend any money or enjoy themselves. For the rest of us, we are constantly trying to strike a balance between enjoying life now and ensuring we have the resources to enjoy life later.

There is no ideal balance for everyone because we all have different goals, needs, resources, expectations, and desires. The hardest part about planning for your financial future is the simple fact that no one knows what's going to happen. No one has it all figured out because no one knows the curve balls life is going to throw at them.

My thoughts about this have changed over the years. I've been a saver for as long as I can remember. So balance for me has been reminding myself that it's okay to spend money on those areas I care about and cut back on everything else. A life with a full bank account but no experiences or enjoyment is pointless. But a life with an empty bank account can steal your enjoyment now and later in life so there are always trade-offs to consider.

You can find information about markets and investing just about everywhere these days. Personal finance advice is now as abundant as it's ever been but the focus is typically on ways to save money. Saving is obviously important but the other side of the equation doesn't get nearly enough attention - spending money. No one ever teaches you about how to spend, or more importantly, prioritize, how you spend.

One of the reasons this is the case is because no one actually enjoys budgeting since the concept generally makes people feel bad about themselves. Yet understanding how and where you spend your money is perhaps one of the most important aspects of a successful financial savings plan.

There are generally two approaches to budgeting:

(1) **Manual.** Track every single item you spend money on down to the last penny to understand where your money goes.

(2) **Autopilot.** Automate as much of your spending and saving as humanly possible and spend whatever is left over.

The manual option is for those who require a full overhaul of their financial ecosystem who don't want to utilize technology in their financial plan. Personal finance guru Dave Ramsey advocates for an envelope-based system where you put all of your cash into different spending categories. Those envelopes could be labeled groceries, clothes, entertainment, gas, etc. And when the money runs out of one envelope, either you're done spending in that category or have to pull from another category. The envelope system is essentially used to control how much you spend in each area of your life.

There is nothing wrong with the manual approach but I prefer the autopilot version because it requires less ongoing maintenance. **Putting your finances on autopilot requires more work up front but the benefits can last a lifetime.** Peter Drucker once said, "Don't make a hundred decisions when one will do." The same applies to automating your finances.

Putting your finances on autopilot requires setting up the following tasks:

- Automatic bill pay for every periodic expense
- Automatic credit card payments to avoid crippling debt, high interest payments, and late fees

- Automatic investment contributions to your retirement and savings accounts
- Automatic debt repayments

The more you can take these decisions out of your own hands the better because it helps cut down on unnecessary late fees and overdraft charges on your bank account. It's estimated the biggest credit card companies make roughly $100 billion a year on late fees and interest charges alone. If you have your accounts on autopilot you don't have to worry about those types of unnecessary charges because every month your credit card will be paid off automatically.

And once you become a true personal finance ninja, you can pay for all of your automatic charges with a credit card that offers rewards so the large financial institutions are actually paying you to use their services. These rewards can come in the form of travel points, cash back and even contributions to investment or savings accounts. The fact that these companies are able to offer rewards to cardholders shows you how much money they make off borrowers who don't pay off their bills on time.

"Pay yourself first" is one of the oldest personal finance rules in the book for a reason - it works. Willpower is fleeting so if your strategy is to save whatever is left over every month you're bound to come up short eventually. Most people simply spend what's available until there are no leftovers. **The trick is to treat your savings like a Netflix subscription that gets paid every month on a set schedule.**

The 401(k) plan is far from perfect but one of the retirement account's best attributes is the built-in convenience. You set either a dollar amount or percentage of your income that will be taken from your paycheck and those funds will never hit your bank account in the first place. It's saved on your behalf automatically before you're ever tempted to spend it. This is crucial because inertia is one of the biggest enemies of behavioral change.

If you don't set these systems up in advance it becomes harder to do so later after you become comfortable with your current level of pay. In countries where the default option for organ transplants is to opt-out of the program (meaning you're automatically signed up unless you tell them otherwise), 90% of people register to donate their organs. In countries where the default option for organ donor programs is to opt-in (meaning you have to sign up on your own), the rate of people registering is just 15%. Defaults are very powerful.

Vanguard performed a comprehensive study of the $1.3 trillion in 401(k) plans they sponsor and discovered those firms that offered an opt-out automatic enrollment for their employees saw savings rates that were 56% higher than those firms who utilized an opt-in approach to sign-up. They also found employees under age 35 who make less than $50,000 a year had a savings rate that was twice as high when their employer used automatic enrollment instead of voluntary enrollment in their retirement plan.

Automating as much of your financial ecosystem as possible frees you up to spend less time on your finances. You simply spend whatever is left over after your retirement contributions and bills have been auto-deducted from your checking account. This allows you to spend money without feeling guilty about it because you've already taken care of the financial necessities. It also forces you to spend more on those things that make you happy and cut back elsewhere. Of course, this strategy still requires some thought about what spending areas truly matter to you. But getting to a point where you're more aware of your priorities can help identify those places where you can cut back on spending to ensure there's less waste in your financial life.

Whichever route you choose, there are enormous benefits to understanding your spending habits because it helps you understand where your priorities lie.

If you can't get your priorities in line, it will be impossible to save for retirement in a meaningful way.

CHAPTER 17. THE HIERARCHY OF RETIREMENT SAVINGS ACCOUNTS

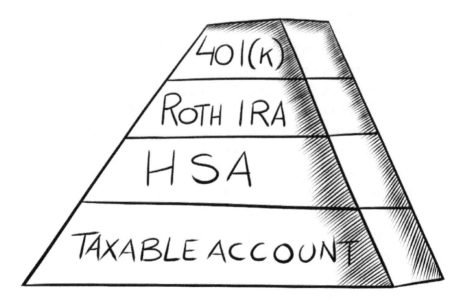

Not every worker is blessed with a high-quality, low-cost workplace retirement plan. Many employers simply don't have the resources or knowledge base to select a plan that's right for their employees. The worst plans come with high administrative costs, mutual funds with high fees and a lack of investment choices to properly diversify your portfolio.

So what are you supposed to do when faced with a subpar plan through no fault of your own?

You could petition your HR department for a change in plans but there's no guarantee they'll listen. Most employers have established relationships and the inertia from going through that process once can often be enough to keep them in a below average retirement plan.

Regardless of how bad your fund options are, you always, always, *always* take the company match if it's offered. That's free money and an automatic return on your savings. Turning down the company match is the equivalent of taking a bonus check from your employer and lighting it on fire. As of 2019, roughly half of the employers in Vanguard's retirement plans offered a company match. The majority of those employers who offered a match would contribute 3% on the first 6% of income saved by the employee. So count yourself lucky if you have this option because simply taking that 3% match gets you pretty darn close to my double-digit savings rate target.

If you have a plan with suitable, low-cost target date or index fund options, terrific, work on slowly increasing your savings rate over time into those types of funds. Many plan sponsors now allow you to automatically escalate your savings rate over time to ease into the process. If you can get to the point where you are maxing your 401(k) that puts you in rarified territory.

If your workplace retirement plan is full of funds with extremely high fees or doesn't have enough choices and does not offer a match, or your employer doesn't offer a retirement plan, the next logical step is to fund your IRA (individual retirement account).

An IRA is similar to a 401(k) in many ways, with the biggest differences being there is a lower contribution limit, you have to open up an account at the fund firm of your choice and there are far more investment options at your disposal. There are also retirement account options for entrepreneurs such as SEP-IRAs and Solo-401(k)s but other than the contribution limits and requirements for signing up for these accounts, they are similar to an IRA.

For both an IRA or 401(k) one of the options people have to consider these days is the traditional or Roth version. The difference between the two comes down when you pay taxes.

Let's assume Jennifer earns a nice round number like $100,000 and saves 15% of her income in her company's 401(k) plan. Each year Jennifer is setting aside $15,000 before receiving a company match. If she were to save that money in a traditional pretax 401(k), this means her taxable income would be $85,000. Jennifer would not pay taxes on that $15,000 until she retires and begins drawing down her portfolio. Assuming her tax rate is 25%, instead of paying $25,000 (25% of $100,000) a year in taxes, she would only pay $21,250 (25% of $85,000 in taxable income), which is a tax deferral of $3,750 per year. Notice I didn't call this a tax savings, because Jennifer will have to pay taxes on these funds eventually, but this is a nice up front benefit of saving money in a tax-deferred retirement account.

Now let's see how things would look if Jennifer decided to save for retirement using a Roth 401(k). Everything would be the same except for the tax treatment. If her tax rate is 25% that means she would pay $25,000 in taxes each year, including taxes on her $15,000 contribution to her Roth 401(k). But when that money comes out of her portfolio at retirement she pays no taxes because she already paid them up front.

This is the type of decision where you shouldn't overthink things. No one has a clue what future tax rates will look like so trying to make a spreadsheet answer to the traditional vs. Roth dilemma is difficult to quantify, especially the further away from retirement you are. If you want to nerd out on tax codes you could probably come up with an optimized strategy to make your decision.

For those who would like to keep things simple, I like the idea of diversifying your tax exposure. So maybe you utilize a traditional 401(k) through your employer but also have a Roth IRA that you make contributions to as well. Or you could use a traditional and Roth 401(k) plan in concert with one another if your employer has both options. That way you earn some tax breaks now and save some tax breaks for future you.

If you have all high interest rate credit card debt paid off, have an emergency savings account set up, max out your 401(k), max out your IRA, you can always move on to a taxable account at a brokerage or fund firm and think about funding other goals such as 529 plans for your kids to save for college or HSAs for healthcare expenses. If you're at this point in your savings journey, congratulations, you're doing better than the vast majority of Americans when it comes to your finances.

Now it's time for the biggest question for savers: When can you retire?

CHAPTER 18.
WHEN CAN I RETIRE?

When you first set out to save and invest your mindset is often stuck on the idea of becoming rich. As you age and priorities shift, that mindset turns into a fear of dying poor.

Do I have enough money saved?

How much will healthcare cost during retirement?

When should I take Social Security?

What if there is a market crash right after I retire?

How can I be sure my money will last?

These are all legitimate questions worth considering but this goes to show you the uncertainties of the retirement planning process don't end once you reach retirement age. Stock market crashes and recessions can be scary to live through, especially for retirees who no longer have the human capital or time to wait out a prolonged downturn. But your biggest risk is not market or economic volatility, but running out of money before you keel over.

Managing your finances in retirement requires a balance between the need for stability in the short term versus the need for growth in the long term. Even a 2% inflation rate would nearly cut your purchasing power in half over 30 years in retirement if you simply buried your money in the backyard. Most investors will be forced to take some risk and accept some volatility in their portfolio to ensure they have enough money to see them through the long haul.

Daniel Kahneman once asked, "How do you understand memory? You don't study memory. You study forgetting." This is how to think about the problem of figuring out how much money you need for retirement as well. How do you understand how much you need for retirement? You don't figure out a number. You figure out how much you spend and save. **It's pointless to try to figure out how**

much you'll need in savings or income if you don't have a good understanding of how much it costs for you to live.

Where you are in your lifecycle will obviously have a lot to do with how you think about these factors. In your younger years, it's almost impossible to plan ahead for the exact amount you'll need based on the exact amount you'll spend during retirement. There are simply too many variables to consider, many of which can and will change by the time you do decide to accept that gold watch and retire.

As you approach retirement you'll have a much better grasp of how much you spend on an annual basis and what your wants, needs, and desires will be in your retirement years. From those numbers, you can come up with a better estimate to determine how much of a nest egg you'll need to cover your annual expenditures from your portfolio.

You'll never be able to figure out how much enough is in terms of your retirement savings if you don't have a deep understanding of your spending. Your monthly burn rate is a pretty good starting point when thinking through how far your savings will take you. And it's not only the things you spend your money on that matter but the things you *don't* spend your money on.

Is your mortgage paid off? Do you have any other outstanding consumer debt? Are you kids off your payroll? The combination of a high savings rate going into retirement along with a dearth of debt obligations can make your savings last much longer than the alternative. Going into retirement with little in the way of debt increases your financial flexibility enormously. High fixed costs are your biggest enemy when seeking financial independence.

Investing during retirement does introduce some new variables and risks to the equation you have to be aware of. Getting a handle on your spending helps but you still have to figure out how much to take from your portfolio each year, which investments to take from and which accounts offer the most tax-efficient withdrawal strategy.

Financial markets never move in a straight line so this process requires some flexibility depending on how things shake out in the markets and how your spending evolves throughout your retirement. Your investment plan doesn't need to change every time stocks rise or fall but you do have to incorporate real world market performance with your built-in expectations. Any useful investment plan takes into account the need for course corrections on occasion. As the old saying goes, "Plans are useless but planning is indispensable."

It will be nearly impossible to implement a sound investment plan if you don't have a handle on your sources of income during retirement. For some people this could simply include Social Security and investment income from their portfolio. Others could have a pension plan, an inheritance, rental income from a second home or a part-time job to supplement their spending needs.

There are all sorts of risks to consider during retirement including outliving your money, inflation, emergencies, unplanned one-time expenses, healthcare costs, the sequence of your investment returns and general market volatility. This is why diversification among stocks, bonds, cash and other assets is so important. It helps you plan for the wide range of outcomes life tends to throw at you.

The financial aspects of retirement can seem overwhelming but the first step in the process boils down to figuring out what you want to do with your life during your retirement years. You'll never be able to figure out your finances if you don't first figure out what you want to buy with your life savings. The entire reason you're saving in the first place is to purchase your freedom. You're buying your own time.

So what are you going to do with that time? Travel? Volunteer? Read more? Spend more time with family? Only work on projects that interest you? Even the greatest retirement planning in the world won't get you very far if you haven't decided how you'll spend your time and money. People often spend decades investing their money without giving a second thought to how they'll invest their time. Studies have shown that experiences and giving back to others often bring the greatest happiness to retirees and help ward off the potential depression which can afflict many who leave the working world.

You can run through all the calculations and spreadsheets you want but life will inevitably get in the way as some of your assumptions will be proven wrong. This is an unfortunate side effect of trying to plan in the face of irreducible uncertainty. In a way, there's a lot of guessing involved in the process. This is why financial planning is a process and not an event. You don't simply set a course of action and follow that exact plan for your remaining days. Financial plans should be open-ended because there will always be corrective actions, updates, changes in strategy and difficult decisions that have to be made.

There's never a perfect time to retire just like there's no such thing as a perfect portfolio. If you have your personal finances in order, understand how much it costs you to live, where your income will be coming from during retirement and how you'll spend your days, that's a pretty good start.

But what if you want to ensure you'll retire a millionaire? Up next is a look at what's required.

CHAPTER 19.
HOW TO BECOME A
401(K) MILLIONAIRE

The current number of millionaires in the United States is around 5% of the population or 1 out of every 20 people. There's nothing special about the million dollar mark per se but it's a wealth threshold people have held in high esteem ever since novelist and future Prime Minister of Britain, Benjamin Disraeli, first used the term in 1827.

Fidelity Investments is one of the largest retirement fund companies on the planet, managing more than $3 trillion in 401(k) and IRA assets. Only 1% or so of Fidelity's plan participants have $1 million or more in these accounts.

Becoming a 401(k) millionaire is unusual because it's not easy. But how feasible is it? Let's take a look at the numbers. Using the maximum contribution amount of $19,500 in the year 2020, these are the investment returns required to reach a million dollars by age 65:

Starting Age	Required Return For $1 Million at Age 65
30	2.0%
35	3.0%
40	4.8%
45	7.7%
50	12.8%

Assumes $19,500 invested annually

If you've been following along throughout the book, it's not a ground-breaking discovery to point out how helpful it is to begin saving at a young age. The required returns to hit $1 million for someone who maxes out their 401(k) in their 30s is a fairly low hurdle rate. Wait to start saving until you're in your late-40s or 50s and it's much harder to get to seven figures because your required rate of return is higher.

Obviously, maxing out your retirement contributions is not an easy task, especially in your 30s. Student loans, a house down payment, kids and everything else life throws at you means few people have the means to max out their retirement savings at that stage in life.

According to Vanguard just 4% of savers in their defined contribution plan who earn $50,000 a year max out their 401(k). For those making between $50k and $100k that number jumps to 11% of participants. And 32% of people making $100k or more max out their tax-deferred savings.

It's also tough to go from 0 to 60 and begin maxing out your retirement account without slowly building up to that level. Few individuals or households have the means to max out their retirement savings straight out of the gate.

Let's say you want to take advantage of the power of small wins by slowly increasing the amount you save over time until that max contribution level is hit.

If you were to begin saving at age 30 at the following monthly amounts and increasing those contributions by $100 a month each year until you reach the max, these are the corresponding required returns:

Initial Monthly Savings	Initial Annual Savings	Required Returns
$250	$3,000	3.3%
$350	$4,200	3.1%
$450	$5,400	2.9%
$550	$6,600	2.7%
$650	$7,800	2.5%

Assumes you add $1,200/year ($100/month) to each year until $19,500 max is reached

Start at age 30 and stop at age 65

Here's the same exercise starting at age 35:

Initial Monthly Savings	Initial Annual Savings	Required Returns
$250	$3,000	5.1%
$350	$4,200	4.7%
$450	$5,400	4.4%
$550	$6,600	4.2%
$650	$7,800	4.0%

Assumes you add $1,200/year ($100/month) each year until $19,500 max is reached
Start at age 35 and stop at age 65

And once more using age 40 as the starting point:

Initial Monthly Savings	Initial Annual Savings	Required Returns
$350	$4,200	7.4%
$450	$5,400	6.9%
$550	$6,600	6.5%
$650	$7,800	6.2%
$750	$9,000	5.9%

Assumes you add $1,200/year ($100/month) each year until $19,500 max is reached
Start at age 40 and stop at age 65

The required returns are surprisingly low in these examples but everything looks easier on paper than in real life, especially when money is involved. **Saving, investing and getting your personal finances in order are always more of an exercise in psychology than math.** It would be irrational of me to suggest that *everyone* should be able to become a 401(k) millionaire because some families or individuals are simply never going to be able to save this much money on a regular basis.

Whether you become a 401(k) millionaire or not, there are some lessons from this data:

- **Consistency matters but life is inconsistent.** Consistently saving money from a relatively young age over time can make up for a lack of investment acumen or lower than average returns from financial markets. But consistently saving money in a linear fashion over time is probably one of the hardest things to do because life is inconsistent. If you're a robot, saving up a large nest egg should be an easy feat. Unfortunately, it's not. Life is full of curveballs. Plan accordingly.

- **Change can disrupt your retirement plans.** The only way numbers like this work is if you never stop making contributions to your 401(k). They also don't work for those who take out loans from their 401(k) or cash out their 401(k) when they change jobs or pay penalties for making early withdrawals from their 401(k). Turning a little money into a lot of money is about patience but patience is useless without a side of discipline and consistency.

- **"Enough" means different things to different people.** There is no perfect number when it comes to retirement planning. The end goal will always depend on your circumstances, standard of living, spending preferences, lifestyle choices and relationship with money.

Most of the saving exercises in this book are meant to drive home the benefits of saving from a young age but all is not lost if you got a late start on retirement saving.

In the next chapter, we'll look at what you need to do if you waited to get started with retirement planning until your 40s or 50s.

CHAPTER 20.
WHAT IF YOU GET A
LATE START SAVING
FOR RETIREMENT?

There are many reasons so many people in the older age bracket are so ill-prepared financially for retirement. Some people simply don't make enough money to set aside enough for their later years. Others have bad luck in their career, horrible financial role models, poor personal finance habits or a lack of knowledge when it comes to money management. As someone with three young children, I can also see how many parents would put their children first when it comes to their spending priorities.

Whatever the reason, there are a number of people who wish they would have started saving when they were younger but didn't. Beginning the process of saving for retirement in your 40s or 50s isn't ideal but it's not a lost cause either. If you got a late start on retirement planning there are still steps you can take to fund your post-working years. You just have to make some potentially uncomfortable moves and stop wasting time. The best time to start saving was 10 years ago but the second best time is today. Don't be discouraged if you're in this place. Many people in this same situation give up saying it's too late but that's not the case.

Older savers do have some potential advantages. You should be in your peak earnings years. Hopefully the kids are out of the house and off your payroll. **Empty-nesters could use the money they were using to fund their children's college or other costs and funnel them into savings.** The same is true if you get to the point where you pay off your mortgage. If you've already been making those debt repayments for many years you can immediately shift those payments to your savings. The government even offers catch-up provisions to employees over the age of 50 (as of 2020 that was an extra $6,500 in a 401(k) and an extra $1,000 in an IRA on top of the standard contribution limits).

You might be tempted to shoot the moon and take on tons of risk with your investments to play catch-up but **saving money is still far more important than how you invest** when we're talking a period of maybe 10-20 years to build up your retirement balance before retiring.

Let's assume Carl and Carla Carlson are both 50 years old with little in the way of retirement savings. The kids are now out of the house so they can supercharge their savings to make up for lost ground. Carl wants to take more risk to make up for their shortfall while Carla would rather increase their savings rate to make up for lost ground.

The Carlson's currently have a household income of $100,000 that will grow at a 2% cost of living adjustment each year. Carla expects their investments to compound at 6% annually and would like to save 20% of their income, while Carl thinks he can do much better than that by trading stocks and saving a little less. Carla thinks Carl is too overconfident in his stock-picking abilities and would rather save more money than taking on a riskier investment strategy.

The couple wants to retire by age 65 or 70 but are unsure how far their savings can get them in such a short amount of time. Let's look at an example which shows their current plan, one with a higher savings rate and one where Carl's stock picks knock it out of the park:

Savings Rate	Investment Return	After 10 Years	After 15 Years	After 20 Years
10%	6%	$143,977	$264,029	$432,112
20%	6%	$287,954	$528,058	$864,225
10%	12%	$192,013	$418,634	$826,370

Assumes $100k income growing at 2% per year

Even if Carl knocked it out of the park in his Robinhood account and doubled up Carla's 6% return target, a higher savings rate would have still led to better results. A doubling of the Carlson's savings rate from 10% to 20% led to a better outcome than a doubling of their investment returns from 6% to 12%, even over a two decade period. And chances are Carl is not the second-coming of Warren Buffett so increasing their savings rate is far easier than increasing their investment returns.

Taking more risk in your portfolio doesn't guarantee you anything in the markets. The market won't give you good returns just because you need them. Your savings rate is something you control while no one controls the returns thrown off by the financial markets. A more likely scenario is by taking more risk Carl would actually harm the performance of their savings because the track record of professional, let alone amateur, stock-pickers is so poor.

Saving at an early age is important because it helps you build solid financial habits and allows compound interest to snowball your money over time. But saving is probably even more important for those who are behind on their retirement savings because you don't have as long to allow compounding to do its thing.

Now this doesn't mean your time horizon as an investor is done right when you retire. According to the Social Security administration, a couple retiring today has a 50% chance that at least one of them will live into their 90s. You could still have two to three decades to manage your money during your post-work years. It's just that your time as an earner and saver may have a shelf life if you don't work during retirement.

There are other ways for Carl and Carla to extend the life of their portfolio. Investment expert Charles Ellis found delaying your retirement from age 62 to age 70 could reduce your required savings rate by more than 50%. Working longer not only allows you to save more money, it allows that money to compound for longer, lowers the number of years your portfolio needs to last during retirement and potentially allows you to delay taking Social Security payments. Delaying Social Security benefits from age 62 to age 70 can increase your monthly benefit by more than 70%. Not everyone wants to work longer but for those who are willing and able it can drastically increase your odds of success in retirement.

Whether you got a late start to retirement or not, knowing when you can retire is a struggle for everyone.

Up next is the most important retirement program in America.

CHAPTER 21.
WHAT ABOUT
SOCIAL SECURITY?

The Great Depression and its aftermath in the 1930s left pension plans and households financially decimated. The unemployment rate climbed as high as 25% and many people lost their life savings. There was no such thing as a social safety net at the time so people were more or less on their own.

Upon signing the Social Security Act in 1935, President Franklin D. Roosevelt proclaimed, "We have tried to frame a law which will give some measure of protection to the average citizen and to his family against the loss of a job and against poverty-ridden old age." Since that time nearly $8 trillion has been paid out to citizens in Social Security. Full retirement is age 66 for people born between 1943 and 1954 and gradually increases to 67 for people born in 1960 and later. You can choose to take Social Security at age 62 but the benefit will be about 25% less than what it would be at full retirement age. Waiting until age 70 to start collecting would result in a 30% increase from the amount starting at full retirement age. Every year you wait past 62 increases your annual Social Security payment by about 8% per year.

Social Security is the largest single program in the Federal Budget most years. And while Social Security isn't a perfect retirement solution it has helped millions of people live in dignity in retirement. The average earner can expect the program to replace roughly 30-40% of their income. And because the program is progressive, those benefits replace a larger share for low income workers, roughly two to three times higher for workers in the lowest 20% of wages than the highest 20% of earners. This can help bridge the gap for those who have little in the way of retirement savings or are worried their financial assets won't be enough. In fact, if you were to capitalize the value of the average Social Security payments over the life of a recipient, the present value of that income stream would be somewhere in the $200,000 to $300,000 range depending on the discount rate used.

I know what many of you are thinking - *That's great and all, Ben, but Social Security is a Ponzi scheme! The money is going to run out by the time I need it. It's a house of cards!*

I hate to be the bearer of good news, but that's probably not going to happen.

Yes, people are living longer and many of the 73 million Baby Boomers are either already retired, getting ready to retire or planning to retire in the coming years. That's going to put some strain on the system. The Social Security board of trustees puts out an annual report with updated stats and estimates to show how the program is holding up. They predict by 2034 there will be more retirees taking money out than workers putting money in through payroll taxes. From 1974-2008 there were somewhere between 3.2 and 3.4 workers for every beneficiary receiving social security. By 2035, when the baby boomers generation will largely be retired, they estimate that number will be more like 2.3 workers supporting every beneficiary.

So it's understandable why many people are worried the cookie jar will be empty by the time they get to retirement.

But just because there will be fewer workers supporting the program doesn't mean the fund will be completely depleted. The CBO estimated Social Security payments will still be close to 80% covered by payroll taxes. The government could decide to simply cut social security benefits by 20% when this happens but I doubt that will happen.

Here's why:

Too many people rely on Social Security. The Center on Budget and Policy Priorities estimates 3 out of 10 elderly Americans would be more or less broke without the help of Social Security and more than 10 million elderly Americans have been lifted out of poverty because of the program. Social Security also acts as one of the biggest sources of retirement income for many Americans. Roughly half of all senior citizens get at least 50% of their retirement income from

Social Security. Around 1 in 4 seniors receive 90% of retirement income from this program.

How many politicians in their right mind would ever conceive of cutting benefits for their biggest voting base? It would be political suicide.

There are simple fixes to the program. The government could simply increase the deficit to continue funding social security in the future but there are some simple fixes that could make sense to put it on a sounder financial footing. The way your benefit is calculated is based on how much you earn over the course of your career and the age at which you begin taking benefits. To avoid angering seniors, the government could increase the retirement age for younger people below a certain cut-off point. Or they could adjust the earnings cap, payroll taxes or the cost of living adjustment.

There are a number of levers to pull that would alleviate some strain on the program or the government could always cut back their spending in other areas (Who am I kidding? They'll probably just pile on more debt).

Government spending is only constrained by political will. Government spending is not constrained by some line in the sand but by political will. We literally cannot run out of money in the United State because we can print more of it with the push of a button. So the only way Social Security will not be there for young people is if the government decides it's not a priority.

It's possible your benefit will be reduced in the coming decades or you'll have to wait a little longer to start drawing distributions but I feel fairly safe telling people they can plan on receiving something from Social Security in retirement as long as they continue paying payroll taxes.

Social Security is one of the most important retirement accounts in the country but there's another retirement plan that's vital to America's teachers.

A deep dive on the pros and cons of 403(b) accounts is up next.

CHAPTER 22.
THE ABCS OF 403(B)S
FOR TEACHERS

The 401(k) plan is the most well-known of workplace retirement plans in the United States but there is a similar option for nonprofit organizations called a 403(b). Participants in 403(b) retirements plans include public school teachers, school administrators, government employees and healthcare workers at hospitals.

The biggest difference between the two is that many 403(b) plans are non-ERISA, meaning they are not required to comply with many of the regulations set out in the Employee Retirement Income Security Act (ERISA). This is not ideal for workers in 403(b) plans because it removes basic protections for participants and invites bad actors to take advantage of people who don't know any better. This is most notable among public school teachers.

The 403(b) has actually been around longer than the 401(k), as it was started in 1958. Unfortunately, that's about the only leg up it has on its counterpart. The lack of regulations means 403(b)s have little involvement from their employers in most cases and contain far more insurance products. Insurance products were the only investment option allowed until a rule change in 1974 opened the door for mutual funds. And since the schools themselves have no fiduciary duty, which is simply the legal obligation to act in the best interest of participants and their beneficiaries, many teachers and other 403(b) participants are taken advantage of.

Annuities can be a useful insurance product under the right circumstances. The problem is tax-deferred retirement accounts are not the right account for these products, the fees tend to be egregiously high, and most teachers don't understand how their life savings are being treated in these products. The people pitching annuities know how to prey on the fears of our educators who don't have anyone looking out in their best interests. The firms who sell these products oftentimes pay for the administrative fees in exchange for making it on the preferred vendor list. This is a wolf-in-sheep's clothing act to gain access to teachers to sell them products that would never be allowed in 401(k) plans. An annuity wrapper might be the most expensive way to own a mutual fund on the planet. And these products are created to produce income for investors, not accumulate wealth.

Retirement consulting firm Aon Hewitt estimates 76% of 403(b) plan assets for teachers reside in fixed or variable annuities with the remaining 24% in mutual funds. This is not normal. Instead of investing in simple target date or index funds that you can find in any 401(k) plan, teachers are being hawked complex annuities that some of the best and brightest minds in finance couldn't hope to decipher.

The fees on these annuities can run in the range of 2-3% annually, with up to 5% commissions for the salesperson and yet another 5-7% in early surrender charges if you want to sell out of the product early. Even the best hedge funds in the world don't have these types of terms. The only way to understand these products requires reading prospectuses that are hundreds of pages long, which are written by lawyers to protect the insurance companies, not the teachers investing in them.

Beyond lax regulations on these plans, there are simply too many investment options for teachers to choose from.

In 2000, psychologists published a study on jam, of all things, that helps explain why too many options can be detrimental to retirement investment selections. The study took place at a grocery store, where shoppers would see different displays of upscale jam depending on the day. One day, they would be presented with a $1 coupon for 24 different types of gourmet jam while another day showed just 6 flavors. The larger display tended to garner more interest from shoppers but they were just one-tenth as likely to follow through with a purchase than those who saw a smaller display.

This is a paradox of choice - we assume more is better but often it leads to a paralysis by analysis. This is especially true in an area like retirement planning where the participants are generally at an information disadvantage. The insurance industry says teachers deserve more choices but this violates every law in behavioral finance.

Since most teachers are buying annuities using individual contracts, there are no economies of scale to negotiate lower fees like 401(k) plan sponsors are able to do. When you add it all up, Aon Hewitt figures **teachers are paying $10 *billion* in excess fees** in comparison to a typical 401(k) plan.

So what can teachers do to save themselves?

Don't assume your pension will completely cover you. Having a pension puts teachers in a better position than most but it may not be enough to cover your retirement years. Most pensions do not come with an inflation adjustment so a two to three decade retirement could see their purchasing power devastated over time by rising prices.

Many teachers also leave the profession before they're fully vested. For this very reason, less than one-third of all teachers participate in a 403(b) to begin with. And assuming a pension will cover all of your expenses in retirement means you could be wasting your most important saving years and leaving money on the table by not allowing compound interest to do its thing over the long haul.

This is especially true for young teachers who don't have access to the cushy benefits many older teachers had before them. Many state pension plans are badly underfunded making future benefit cuts more likely. It's also worth noting, teachers in 15 states aren't covered by Social Security. Like it or not, you are still responsible for your own retirement planning.

Invest only in low-cost fund options you understand. If you don't understand something, don't invest in it. Complex problems don't always require complex solutions. In the investing game, that means keeping things simple, picking funds with low costs that are easy to understand and never placing your money in something you couldn't explain to a 6-year-old. It's relatively simple to add these options to a plan, so go to your business office and demand low-cost fund options if they're not available.

Save and invest outside of the 403(b) plan. If your 403(b) plan offers a match, by all means don't turn down that free money. But there's no law that says you can't invest outside of your school's 403(b) plan by opening up an IRA or taxable account. It's not as convenient but after setting it up the entire saving and investment process can be automated with a few short clicks at the majority of reputable fund firms, robo-advisors or online brokerages. This is a much better option than high-priced annuities.

There is an assumption by many investors that those who work in the finance industry are required to have the client's best interests at heart when giving financial advice. Unfortunately for teachers this isn't always the case. Caveat emptor.

Now let's take a look at my 20 rules of personal finance.

CHAPTER 23.
THE 20 RULES OF
PERSONAL FINANCE

Picture yourself getting ready for a Clark Griswold-style family summer road trip.

You have an itinerary all laid out for every stop along the way including the hotels you'll stay at, the sites you'll see and even the Yelp reviews for the various restaurants you plan to eat at on your trip.

The day finally arrives when you plan to take off. The anticipation for a trip is often more exciting than the vacation itself so the entire family is hyped up and ready to go.

Everyone piles into the family minivan, ready to go until someone realizes dad forgot to fill up the gas tank, no one packed their suitcases, someone forgot to pack the snacks and there isn't a single iPad on board to keep the kids happy in the backseat.

The finance equivalent here is coming up with the world's greatest investment strategy without realizing the importance of personal financial planning first. Yes, investing is important if you would like to compound your wealth over time, but it doesn't matter if you're the second coming of Warren Buffett if you can't save money and get your personal finances in order first.

The whole point of this book is to drive home the importance of personal finance and saving but just to sum things up before a concluding chapter, I wanted to provide Ben's 20 rules of personal finance to hammer home these points:

1. Avoid credit card debt like the plague. The first rule of personal finance is never carry a credit card balance. Credit card borrowing rates are egregiously high and paying those rates is an easy way to negatively compound your net worth. Not all debt is necessarily bad but credit card debt is by far the worst. If you carry credit card debt for a prolonged period of time, you're not ready to invest your money in the markets.

2. Building credit is important. Likely the biggest expense over your lifetime will be interest costs on your mortgage, car loans and student loans. Having a solid credit score can save you tens or even hundreds of thousands of dollars by lowering your borrowing costs. So use credit cards to build a solid credit history, but always pay off the balance each month. Putting all of your automated bills on a card that's automatically paid off each month is a good place to start.

3. Income is not the same as savings. There is a huge difference between making a lot of money and becoming wealthy because your net worth is more important than how much money you make. It's amazing how many people don't realize this simple truth. Having a high income does not automatically make you rich; having a low income does not automatically make you poor. All that matters is how much of your income you set aside, not how much you spend. Anyone can spend money to appear wealthy, but true wealth comes from the absence of spending in the form of saving.

4. Saving is more important than investing. Pay yourself first is such simple advice, but so few people do this. The best investment decision you can make is setting a high savings rate because it gives you a huge margin of safety in life. You have no control over the level of interest rates, stock market performance or the timing of recessions and bear markets but you can control your savings rate.

5. Live below your means, not within your means. The only way to get ahead financially is to consistently stay behind your own earnings power. Living within or above your means is how you end up going from paycheck to paycheck without every truly building wealth. The only way to get ahead is by living *below* your means and setting aside a portion of your income for the future. Delayed gratification is poor branding so just think about this in terms of the time you can buy yourself in the future to do what you want, when you want to do it.

6. If you want to understand your priorities look at where you

spend money each month. You have to understand your spending habits if you ever wish to gain control of your finances. The goal is to spend money on things that are important to you but cut back everywhere else. And if you pay yourself first you don't have to worry about budgeting, you just spend whatever's leftover on the things that truly matter to you.

7. Automate everything. The best way to save more, avoid late fees, and make your life easier is to automate as much of your financial life as possible. The goal is to make the big decisions up front so you don't need to waste so much time and energy tending to your finances. It probably takes me an hour a month to keep track of everything because the majority of my family's financial life is on autopilot.

8. Get the big purchases right. I know I shouldn't be so judgmental but whenever I see $50-$70k SUVs on the road or enormous McMansions the first thing that pops into my head is, "I wonder how much they have saved for retirement?" Personal finance experts love to debate the minutiae of brown bag lunches and lattes but the most important purchases in terms of keeping your finances in order will be the big ones - housing and transportation. Overextending yourself on these two purchases can be a killer because they represent fixed costs and come with more ancillary expenses than most people realize.

9. Build up your liquid savings account. I don't even like calling it an emergency savings account anymore because most of the time these "emergencies" are things you should plan on happening periodically. Your monthly spending levels should take into account the fact that there are infrequent, yet predictable expenses you'll need to take care of on occasion. Weddings, vacations, car repairs and health scares never occur on a set schedule but you can plan on paying for these events by setting aside small amounts of money each month to better prepare yourself when life inevitably gets in the way.

10. Cover your insurable needs. This is another personal finance margin of safety item. My friend and colleague Jonathan Novy likes to remind me that people buy insurance because there will be a financial impact on their business or family if they were to die or become disabled. The idea is to measure that impact in dollars, and if possible, insure against it. Just remember that insurance is about protecting wealth, not building it.

11. Always get the match. I can't tell you how many times I've talked to people who aren't saving enough in their 401(k) plan to get the employer match. That's like turning down a portion of your paycheck each payday. I'd like to see more people max out their retirement contributions, but at a minimum you should *always* save enough to get the match so you're not leaving free money on the table.

12. Save a little more each year. Few people have the means to immediately reach my goal of saving 10% to 20% of their income each year so the trick is to increase your savings rates every time you get a raise so you'll never even notice you had more money to begin with. Avoiding lifestyle creep can be difficult, but that's how you build wealth. And the sooner you begin setting money aside, the less you end up realizing it never made it to your checking account to be spent in the first place.

13. Choose your friends, neighborhood and spouse wisely. Robert Cialdini has written extensively on the concept of social proof and how we mirror the actions of others to gain acceptance. Trying to keep up with spendthrift friends or neighbors is a never-ending game with no true winners. Find people to spend your life with who have similar money views as you and it will save you a lot of unnecessary stress, envy and wasteful spending. Don't worry about keeping up with the Joneses as much as following your own path.

14. Talk about money more often. It takes all of 5 minutes before I hear about politics in almost any conversation these days, but somehow money is still a taboo subject. Talk to your spouse about money. Ask others for help. Don't allow financial problems to linger and get worse. Money is a topic that impacts almost every aspect of your life in some way. It's too important to ignore and sweep under the rug.

15. Material purchases won't make you happier in the long run. There is something of a short term dopamine hit we get through retail therapy but it eventually wears off. Buying stuff won't make you happier or wealthier because true wealth is all of the stuff you don't waste money on. Experiences give you a better bang for your buck and time spent with the people you love is one of the best investments you can make.

16. Read a book or 10. There are countless personal finance books out there. If it bores you to death then at least skim through a few and pick out the best pieces of advice from a few different sources to test out. This stuff should be taught in every high school and college, but it isn't. So you have to take the initiative. No one is going to care more about your money decisions than you. Invest some money, time, and energy into yourself. It's the best investment you can make.

17. Know where you stand. Everyone should have a back-of-the-envelope idea of their true net worth. Before knowing where you want to go you have to know where you are. That means adding up all of your assets and subtracting any debts. This way you can set some general expectations about savings rates, market returns and portfolio growth to give yourself some goalposts in the future. Since reality doesn't always sync up with expectations, this allows you to make course corrections along the way to your savings rate, investment strategy or financial plan.

18. Taxes matter. Everyone should try to do their own taxes at least once just to understand how it all works. It can be maddeningly complicated, but it can help you save money over time if you know where to look. Take advantage of as many tax breaks as you can and always understand your personal tax situation. Taxes should never act as the be-all-end-all when making saving and investment decisions, but they definitely deserve a seat at the table. The biggest lay-ups in this category include taking advantage of as many tax-deferred savings vehicles as humanly possible and keeping your trading to a minimum when investing in taxable accounts to avoid paying higher short term capital gains taxes.

19. Make more money. Saving and/or cutting back is a great way to get ahead, but it's an incomplete strategy if you're not trying to earn more by enhancing your career. Too many people are stuck in the mindset that there's nothing they can do to get a better job, take on more responsibilities or earn higher pay. That's nonsense. You must learn how to sell yourself, improve your skills and negotiate a higher income over time. A $10k raise could be worth hundreds of thousands of dollars over the course of your career.

20. Don't think about retirement, but financial independence. The goal shouldn't be about making it to a certain age so you can ride off into the sunset, but rather getting to the point where you don't have to worry about money anymore. Time is the most important asset in the world because you can't manufacture more of it.

Retirement is a concept that is still evolving and no one knows how they'll feel once they reach that age. Becoming financially independent allows you to make decisions about how you spend your time on your own terms.

CONCLUSION: LET ME CONVINCE YOU TO KEEP IT SIMPLE

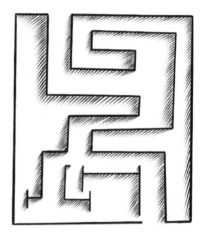

In the 1840s a Hungarian physician named Ignaz Semmelweis noticed a large discrepancy in mortality rates for new mothers during childbirth in the two maternity wards in his hospital. While working at a hospital in Vienna, Semmelweis realized the doctors' maternity ward had three times the mortality rate as the babies being delivered in the midwives' maternity ward.

The biggest difference between the two wards is how the two groups of hospital workers spent their downtime. You see the doctors and medical students experimented on cadavers in the morgue. The midwives did not. After working on the dead bodies the doctors and students didn't wash their hands, thus transferring all sorts of germs to the new mothers during childbirth.

Semmelweis's recommendation to have the doctors begin washing their hands was initially ridiculed by the medical community because this flew in the face of established opinions held at the time. Germ theory had been proposed in the 19th century but many experts still believed in the spontaneous generation of germs and bacteria. Obviously, Semmelweis was proven right eventually but it took time for people to change their minds. The life expectancy for new mothers rose dramatically. There is now a greater proportion of 20-year-old Americans who have a living grandmother than had a living mother in the year 1900.

It's amazing how something as simple as washing your hands can lead to such a vast improvement in the quality of life. This is a good reminder that **advice doesn't have to be complicated to be effective**.

While I can't prove this as 100% fact, here are the reasons why I believe simple beats complex in the investment world:

It's easier to be fooled by randomness and complexity. If you torture the data long enough it's bound to tell you exactly what you want to hear. Complexity invites data-mining, over-optimization and seeing correlation where there is no causation. Right or wrong, simplifying makes it harder to game your own system.

Complexity is about tactics; simplicity is about systems. Tactics come and go but an overarching philosophy about the way the world works can help you make better decisions in many different scenarios. Simple doesn't go out of style.

Simple is harder. You have to fight to keep things simple because our natural human impulses make us susceptible to stories and narratives. Simplicity is more of a psychological exercise while complexity is more about trying to outsmart the competition.

Complexity can lead to unanticipated consequences. Simplicity was once described to me as the art of thoughtful reduction. Sherlock Holmes once said, "If you eliminate the impossible, whatever remains, however improbable, must be the truth." Complexity, on the other hand, opens you up to far more possibilities and surprises, and not always in a good way.

Complexity can give you an illusion of control. As a coping mechanism, people look to avoid stress by giving themselves the illusion of control. Certainty makes us feel more comfortable but really it's an illusion. Investors seek out a feeling of certainty and control, even if it means being wrong. Simplifying is about focusing on what you can control and understanding what you cannot.

Complex problems don't require complex solutions. It's difficult to get people to buy into simplicity because it's hard to believe that complex problems don't require complex solutions. We all want to believe that the Holy Grail of investment sophistication exists and if we can only find the secret sauce all of our problems will be solved. This is why get rich quick schemes will always find an audience.

Simple is easier to understand. It's hard to put a value on the ability to understand exactly what you're doing and why. Simplicity allows for more transparency. It's easier to set reasonable expectations. Charlie Munger once said, "Simplicity has a way of improving performance through enabling us to better understand what we are doing."

Maybe the title of this book was a tad misleading. You won't find *everything* you need to know about saving for retirement in these pages. But get the simple stuff right and you're 95% of the way there. Everything else will only make small differences around the edges. If you get just 3 big things right when it comes to your money decisions you'll be better off than the vast majority of Americans:

> **(1) Save a double digit percentage of your income.** There are no guarantees in life or finances but saving a decent chunk of your income is one way to allow some room for error. If you can't get to this goal right away, slowly increase your savings rate over time so you can see some small wins and work up to it.

> **(2) Automate as much as humanly possible.** Automate your bill payments. Automate savings from your paycheck or checking account. Automatically increase your savings rate every year. And make your investment strategy as rules-based as possible.

> **(3) Get out of your own way.** This is the hardest one for most people. Knowledge alone is not enough to change your ingrained human nature or the lesser version of yourself.

Could you do better by implementing a more complex approach to saving and investing for retirement? Sure. There are people who have done so and succeeded. But you have better things to do with your time. Projects to work on. Spending time with your kids. Having dinner or drinks with friends. Creating a new business. Watching Netflix. You don't want to spend all of your time debating the minutiae of retirement planning and personal finance.

It's impossible to give blanket financial advice because so much of it boils down to circumstance, personality, station in life and your relationship with money.

However, I am confident in saying that if you can figure out a way to save 10% to 20% of your income into the financial markets each year, automate that savings and all of your bill payments, increase the amount you save each year by just a little, diversify your investments, and basically leave them alone, you'll be better off financially than the vast majority of retirement savers in America. Everything else is gravy.

Someone once asked Amazon founder and CEO Jeff Bezos the best advice he ever received from Warren Buffett. Bezos asked the Oracle of Omaha, "Your investment thesis is so simple, you're the second richest guy in the world, and it's so simple. Why doesn't everyone just copy you?"

To which Buffett replied, "Because nobody wants to get rich slow."

Getting rich slow is relatively simple. But it is definitely not easy.

******

These are some of the books that have had the biggest impact on my personal finances over the years:

I Will Teach You To Be Rich by Ramit Sethi

The Millionaire Next Door by Thomas Stanley and William Danko

The Little Book of Common Sense Investing by Jack Bogle

Your Money and Your Brain by Jason Zweig

ABOUT THE AUTHOR

Ben Carlson is the Director of Institutional Asset Management at
Ritholtz Wealth Management. Ben has spent his career working with
various nonprofits, institutions and families to help them plan and
invest their money wisely. He is the author of three other books
including *A Wealth of Common Sense: Why Simplicity Trumps Complexity in
Any Investment Plan*, the co-host of the Animal Spirits podcast and
author of the blog, A Wealth of Common Sense.

REFERENCES

Introduction

"The State of American Retirement Savings." Monique Morrissey. Economic Policy Institute. December 2019. https://www.epi.org/publication/the-state-of-american-retirement-savings/

"Report on the Economic Well-Being of U.S. Households in 2017 - May 2018." Board of Governors of the Federal Reserve System https://www.federalreserve.gov/publications/2018-economic-well-being-of-us-households-in-2017-retirement.htm

The Rise and Fall of American Growth: The U.S. Standard of Living since the Civil War. Robert Gordon. Princeton University Press. 2015

"How many states require students to take a personal finance course before graduating from high school? Is it 6 or is it 21?" Tim Ranzetta. Next Gen Personal Finance. February 2020.

Revenue Act of 1978. https://www.finance.senate.gov/imo/media/doc/Hrg95-93.pdf

"Two-Thirds of Americans Aren't Putting Money in Their 401(k)." Ben Steverman. Bloomberg. February 2017. https://www.bloomberg.com/news/articles/2017-02-21/two-thirds-of-americans-aren-t-putting-money-in-their-401-k

"They Saw a Game: A Case Study." Albert H. Hastorf & Hadley Cantril. Journal of Abnormal Psychology. 1954.

Chapter One

The Fifties. David Halberstam. Open Road Media. 2012.

Chapter Two

The Power of Habit: Why We Do What We Do in Life and Business. Charles Duhigg. Random House. 2012.

Atomic Habits: An Easy & Proven Way to Build Good Habits & Break Bad Ones. James Clear Penguin Publishing Group. 2018.

"Temporal Reframing and Savings: A Field Experiment." Hal E. Hershfield, Stephen Shu and Shlomo Benartzi. UCLA. 2018.

Chapter Three
"Retirement Success: A Surprising Look into the Factors that Drive Positive Outcomes." David M. Blanchett and Jason E. Grantz. The ASPPA Journal. 2011.

Chapter Four

"The History of the Air Jordan." Foot Locker
https://www.footlocker.com/history-of-air-jordan.html

Chapter Five

The Investor's Manifesto. William Bernstein. Wiley. 2009.

Chapter Six

"Theo Epstein." The Axe Files. January 2017.

Chapter Ten

"Beyond GE - U.S. workers own too much company stock in retirement plans." Mark Miller. Reuters. July 2018.
https://www.reuters.com/article/us-column-miller-employerstock/column-beyond-ge-u-s-workers-own-too-much-company-stock-in-retirement-plans-idUSKBN1K234Z

Scale: The Universal Laws of Growth, Innovation, Sustainability, and the Pace of Life in Organisms, Cities, Economies, and Companies. Geoffrey West. Penguin Publishing Group. 2017.

"The Agony & The Ecstasy: The Risks and Rewards of a Concentrated Portfolio, Eye on the Market Special Edition." Michael Cembalest
https://www.chase.com/content/dam/privatebanking/en/mobile/docum
ents/eotm/eotm_2014_09_02_agonyescstasy.pdf

"Do Stocks Outperform Treasury Bills?" Hendrik Bessembinder. Journal of Financial Economics. 2018.
https://papers.ssrn.com/sol3/papers.cfm?abstract_id=2900447

Chapter Twelve

"Fund Fees Predict Future Success or Failure." Russel Kinnel. Morningstar. May 2016. https://www.morningstar.com/articles/752485/fund-fees-predict-future-success-or-failure

"Even God Couldn't Beat Dollar Cost Averaging." Of Dollars and Data. Nick Maggiulli. February 2019. https://ofdollarsanddata.com/even-god-couldnt-beat-dollar-cost-averaging/

Chapter Fifteen
The Dorito Effect: The Surprising New Truth About Food and Flavor. Mark Schatzker. Simon & Schuster. 2015.

Mindless Eating: Why We Eat More Than We Think. Brain Wansink. Bantam. 2007.

Chapter Sixteen

"'Opt Out Policies Increase Organ Donation." Francesca Scheiber. Stanford University. https://sparq.stanford.edu/solutions/opt-out-policies-increase-organ-donation

"How America Saves 2020." Brain Alling, Jeffery Clark and David Stinnett. Vanguard. 2020. https://institutional.vanguard.com/ngiam/assets/pdf/has/how-america-saves-report-2020.pdf

"The Invisible Coach." Michael Lewis. Against the Rules. 2020.

Chapter Seventeen

"How America Saves 2020." Brain Alling, Jeffery Clark and David Stinnett. Vanguard. 2020. https://institutional.vanguard.com/ngiam/assets/pdf/has/how-america-saves-report-2020.pdf

"These Workers are Saving the Maximum in Their 401(k) Plans." Darla Mercado. CNBC. August 2019. https://www.cnbc.com/2019/08/01/these-workers-are-saving-the-maximum-in-their-401k-plans.html

Chapter Eighteen

"Fidelity Announces Q1 2018 Retirement Data: Saving Rates Hit Record High and Account Balances Continue to Increase Over Long term." Fidelity. May 2018. https://newsroom.fidelity.com/press-releases/news-details/2018/Fidelity-Announces-Q1-2018-Retirement-Data-Saving-Rates-Hit-Record-High-and-Account-Balances-Continue-to-Increase-Over-Long term/default.aspx

Chapter Nineteen

Falling Short: The Coming Retirement Crisis and What to Do About It. Charles Ellis. Oxford University Press. 2014.

Chapter Twenty

"Historical Background And Development Of Social Security." Social Security Administration. https://www.ssa.gov/history/briefhistory3.html#:~:text=The%20Social%20Security%20Act%20was,a%20continuing%20income%20after%20retirement

"Social Security Replacement Rates and Other Benefit Measures: An In-Depth Analysis." Congressional Budget Office. 2019. https://www.cbo.gov/system/files/2019-04/55038-SSReplacementRates.pdf

Chapter Twenty One

"More isn't always better." Barry Schwartz. Harvard Business Review. June 2006. https://hbr.org/2006/06/more-isnt-always-better

"How 403(b) Plans are Wasting Nearly $10 Billion Annually, and What Can Be Done to Fix It." Daniel Pawlisch and William Ryan. Aon Hewitt Consulting. January 2016. https://www.aon.com/attachments/human-capital-consulting/how-403b-plans-are-wasting-nearly-10billion-annually-whitepaper.pdf

Conclusion

Fewer, Richer, Greener. Laurence Siegel. Wiley. 2019

Made in the USA
Middletown, DE
25 August 2021